POWER TOOLS
FOR ADOLESCENT
LITERACY

Strategies *for* Learning

Jan Rozzelle • Carol Scearce

Solution Tree

555 North Morton Street
Bloomington, IN 47404
(812) 336-7700
FAX: (812) 336-7790
email: info@solution-tree.com
www.solution-tree.com

Printed in the United States of America

ISBN 978-1-934009-35-2

10   9   8   7   6   5   4   3   2   1

Table of Contents

Visit **go.solution-tree.com/literacy** to download all of the reproducibles in this book.

About the Authors

Jan Rozzelle, Ed.D., is executive director of the School-University Research Network and the School Leadership Institute at the School of Education, College of William & Mary. She has devoted her professional life to promoting literacy and leadership and has teaching and administrative experience in grades K–12. Jan has a master's degree in reading and received her doctorate in educational policy, planning, and leadership from the College of William & Mary, where she was awarded the Frances B. and Robert O. Nelson Memorial Scholarship for Character, Commitment, and Achievement and the Dean's Collaborative Leadership Award.

In her current position, Jan directs multiple school improvement partnerships with middle and high schools in Virginia and Tennessee. Her research interests focus on adolescent literacy and teacher and principal instructional leadership development. Jan serves on the Adolescent Literacy Committee of the International Reading Association and is a past president of the Virginia State Reading Association as well as a recipient of the Virginia Reading Teacher of the Year Award. Jan is coauthor of *A Guide to Facilitating Teacher Reflection* (Pacific Learning) and *The Learning Communities Guide to Improving Reading Instruction* (Corwin Press).

Carol Scearce is president of Enlightening Enterprises, a company that provides seminars and workshops to educators throughout Canada and the United States. Her seminars and workshops are practical, active, and humorous. She models what she preaches and gives participants many opportunities to make connections between the workshop and the real world of school.

After teaching grades K–8 for a number of years, Carol received a master's in special education and taught Primary Educable Mentally Retarded for 4 years. During that time, she received the Outstanding Special Educator of the Year Award. She has taught at Georgia Southern University and at Virginia

Commonwealth University. After completing her administration certification, Carol went back to public education to take charge of staff development for a large school system in Chesterfield County, Virginia. She is the author of *122 Ways to Build Teams* (Corwin Press) and many articles.

Preface

> *Do you believe all content teachers should teach literacy?*
>
> *Do you believe adolescents enter middle school using literacy strategies?*

We often begin our content literacy workshops with an anticipation guide that includes these two statements, and we always observe strong reactions from content teachers. English, math, history, and science teachers agree—many adolescents do not know or use literacy strategies. In fact, many teachers do not know or use literacy strategies themselves and believe they just do not have time to teach reading. But seeing is believing. When teachers learn literacy strategies, implement the newly learned strategies in the classroom, and see student learning increase, they realize that literacy strategies are really *learning* strategies. After that, they know they really don't have time *not* to teach literacy.

Literacy strategies empower adolescents because when students actively engage in reading, writing, talking, viewing, and listening, they learn. Our professional mission is to empower teachers with strategies and tools that enable students to read every day in every classroom and write and talk about what they read. With increasing demands from high-stakes assessment for increasing student achievement, effective teachers need a toolbox of instructional strategies to meet the diverse learning needs of adolescents. We dedicate *Power Tools for Adolescent Literacy* to the teachers with whom we've worked and from whom we continue to learn.

We are grateful to Elaine Weber for the vision of the work and to the Jessie Ball duPont Fund, the School-University Research Network, and the School of

Education at the College of William & Mary for endorsing and supporting this work. We are grateful to Gretchen Knapp, our editor, and the team of incredible reviewers who pushed us to the edge with their insightful inspiration—Anne DeFiglio, Robin Fogarty, Valerie Gregory, Tammy Milby, and Carmelita Williams. For steadfast collaboration and generosity, we attribute Carole Geiger, Judy Johnston, and Virginia McLaughlin for enriching our work. We appreciate the teacher leaders on our team, Cindy Bridges, Shandra Dunn, Sarah Harvey, Amy Lamb, and Millie Olson, for making the research come alive with authentic examples from classroom instruction. Last and certainly not least, we acknowledge the patience of our best friends, David O'Brien and Peter Nikas.

Introduction

Using Power Tools to Improve Adolescent Literacy

In many of the schools where we work, one of three students in the typical grade 6–8 classroom reads poorly. For these struggling students, textbooks become harder to read, and learning demands become greater across the grades. Comprehension seems to regress after the elementary grades, and many students hit the reading wall. Our observations of classroom literacy instruction reveal significant gaps between research-based practices and prevalent instruction. Observations in 24 middle schools revealed that middle school teachers:

♦ Engage in modeling as a teaching style only 11% of the time.

♦ Use small group instruction only about 4% of the time, and rarely differentiate small group instruction.

♦ Depend on whole class instruction more than 60% of the time.

♦ Articulate a learning objective about 12% of the time.

♦ Model fluent reading by reading aloud to students only 8% of the time.

♦ Engage students in reading about 19% of the time.

♦ Provide direct teaching of comprehension strategies only 6% of the time.

♦ Depend on worksheets more than any other resource, using them about 55% of the time as compared to journals (6%), content textbooks (14%), and nonfiction text such as articles and trade books (7%).

Middle and high schools lack 1) a comprehensive approach to teaching literacy across the curriculum, 2) high-quality professional development, and 3) classroom resources needed to address a reading motivation problem. Based on our observations, we believe teachers are teaching the only way they know, lecturing to cover content tested on state standardized assessments and using test preparation materials or worksheets. Teachers really *want* to use strategies that engage their students. One teacher commented, "From past experience, I know that students don't read for pleasure and don't comprehend what they do read, and I want to find ways to fix that."

We've been fortunate to work with committed superintendents and principals in the School-University Research Network (SURN), located at the College of William & Mary. SURN responded to the adolescent literacy issue and collaborated to initiate a professional development program for middle school administrators and content area teachers. The SURN model for professional development targets increased use of research-based instructional strategies in the core content areas of English, mathematics, science, and social science. It emphasizes daily reading and writing, consistent direct instruction and student practice of literacy strategies, and the development of critical thinking ability across all content areas.

Teachers have more impact on adolescent learning than any other school factors, and effective teachers own and use a repertoire of effective instructional strategies (Marzano, Pickering, & Pollock, 2001). But assuring success of all adolescents involves more than instructional strategies. Drawing on our best knowledge and experience, we believe that teachers achieve the greatest impact on student achievement when they incorporate the following 12 factors into their practice.

Our Beliefs

We believe that teachers have the greatest impact on student achievement when they:

1. **Expect** all students to learn at unprecedented levels.

2. **Get to know and understand** the adolescent learner.

3. **Schedule time** for students to read every day in every class, and include time to write about and discuss what they read.

4. **Build** a high-performance environment that fosters mutual cooperation, emotional support, and personal and academic growth.

5. **Plan, plan, plan,** using data for continuous improvement.

6. **Collaborate** in teams to design, deliver, and assess effective lessons that integrate high-yield strategies.

7. **Model** comprehension strategies that good readers use every day.

8. **Provide guided practice** that is consistent, systematic, and of high quality, and shift **responsibility** for learning to students.

9. **Read aloud** to students every day to model fluent reading.

10. **Launch** learning through compelling learning objectives.

11. **Organize** learning in a variety of configurations—as individuals, pairs, teams, and whole class—that promote student connectedness to peers, teachers, classrooms, and schools.

12. **Build background knowledge** and teach vocabulary using Marzano's (2004) six steps for instruction.

The Power Tools Conceptual Framework

Our theory of change, based on our underlying beliefs, is illustrated in Figure I-1 (page xvii). Beliefs without actions bring no results, and often a significant gap exists between what we know and what we do in regards to effective teaching—a "knowing-doing gap" (Pfeffer & Sutton, 2000). Many school reforms across the years have created lists of what teachers and principals *should* do, but little change has occurred in most classrooms as a result of these mandates. Figure I-1 reflects critical components of high-quality professional development that result in effective teaching and higher student engagement. This model of practice emphasizes the following:

- ◆ States and districts must provide schools with a "guaranteed and viable curriculum," so that teachers know and teach to the standards on which students are tested.

- ◆ Principals engage in leadership development that 1) focuses on what they should look for in classrooms and 2) supports them in learning strategies for leading school-based professional development and teacher collaboration such as lesson study.

- ◆ Professional development for teachers begins with summer academies and workshops and focuses on the *how* of effective teaching. Teachers see research-based strategies in action as experts model how to implement and teach strategies.

- ◆ Follow-up support aids transfer of newly learned strategies into classroom practice and assesses teacher needs and responds with just-in-time coaching.

- ◆ Peer-coaching experiences provide stepping stones to building collaborative learning communities when teachers support each other in transferring newly learned strategies.

- ◆ Collaborative lesson planning and lesson study engage teachers in integrating tools and strategies in effective lesson plans. Teachers meet at least twice a month to design, implement, and assess lessons.

- ◆ Lesson fairs recognize the accomplishments of teachers and disseminate effective lessons across grades, disciplines, schools, districts, and even regions.

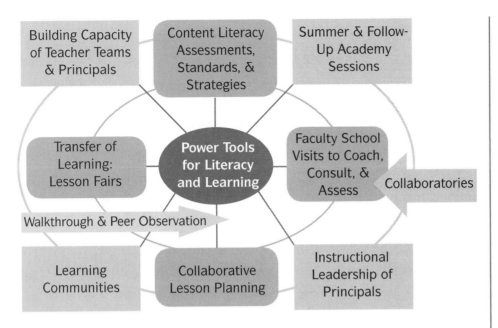

Figure I-1. SURN Adolescent Literacy Professional Development Model

Who Should Use This Book?

In 2005, we were invited to lead a summer academy for teams of teachers and principals from middle and high schools in Richmond, Virginia. To help increase the buy-in of the participants in the change effort, we adopted Richmond City Schools' motto: "To be good is not enough when you dream of being great." We introduced Power Tools to help *good* teachers refine their lessons by integrating strategies that *great* teachers use to achieve high levels of learning. In Richmond and dozens of other schools, this book serves as a resource for:

♦ New teachers beginning the profession who need tools to start their first day

♦ Career switchers who lack background experience in pedagogy and methods

♦ Experienced content teachers interested in ways to increase learning

♦ Principals who want to know what to look for in all core content classrooms

♦ Staff developers who plan professional development for schools and districts

♦ School-based coaches supporting new teachers

♦ Groups of teachers participating in professional book clubs or study groups

How to Use This Book

Teachers and administrators may use this book in any order that fits their needs. For example, if district mandates prioritize vocabulary, start with chapter 4 to acquire tools and strategies for teaching and learning vocabulary. Or start with the Survey of Literacy and Learning on page xx to direct your reading.

Each chapter presents a toolbox of Power Tools strategies for promoting critical thinking and learning across content areas. We provide a short general introduction to the strategies, some key facts, and a few excellent and readily available books for learning more about the focus of each chapter.

Each strategy follows a simple question-and-answer format. We describe the strategy, tell why it's useful, and explain how to use it with step-by-step instructions. Where possible, we provide examples and reproducible templates to assist you in implementing Power Tools in your classroom. Visit **go.solution-tree.com/literacy** to download PDFs of these templates.

The end of each chapter includes a list of all the tools and strategies in the chapter to encourage you to reflect on how you can transfer their knowledge into practice—how you can use the material—by answering the following questions:

♦ *What do I NOT want to try?*

♦ *How can I add this to an existing lesson?*

♦ *What different standards can I use it with?*

♦ *What tool can I change or use another way?*

The Reflection and Application section can be used by an individual teacher, a team of teachers, or an entire staff at a faculty meeting. If your school has set up professional learning communities to study and encourage literacy, this section could be used as part of the discussion. For example, if your team has collected data on the knowledge base of your students' comprehension strategies and learned that the students are not proficient, then you could open a meeting with a review of chapter 2. Next, you could each review the strategy and tool list, answer the reflection questions, and each select one tool to use in your classroom. Afterwards, the team can regroup to discuss the pros and cons of each teacher's experience, what impact the tool had on learning, what you would tell another teacher about using the tool or strategy, and so forth. Going forward, your team could share the strategies and tools you are using at a monthly faculty meeting.

The appendix provides additional tools and information to aid transfer of the strategies and tools into your daily practice. We include an article on the essential elements of literacy instruction that teams can read and discuss in a professional book club. Because we believe that collaborative lesson study results in better lessons and increased learning, we offer a checklist for a template for lesson planning.

Now we encourage you to "let your fingers do the walking"! We hope you *have fun* with this book—and with your students as you implement the tools and strategies and watch them learn!

Survey of Literacy and Learning

Assess your knowledge of the Power Tools listed in the left column. Check the box that indicates your level of knowledge. Then use the results to identify several strategies that you wish to learn about and write a learning goal statement(s).

Power Tool	Clueless	Heard of It	Know It	Could Teach It
Student Learning Survey				
3-2-1 Biography Poem				
People Search				
Literacy History Timeline				
Reading and Writing Interest Inventory				
Class Routine Chart				
The Effort T-Chart				
Let Your Fingers Do the Walking				
Community Learning Walls				
Goal Setting				
Specific Feedback				
Checklist for Student Self-Assessment				
Cooperative and Partnered Learning				
The Magnificent Seven Comprehension Strategies				
Explicit Comprehension Instruction				
Comprehension Bookmarks				

Power Tools for Adolescent Literacy ♦ Copyright © 2009 Solution Tree Press
www.solution-tree.com ♦ Visit **go.solution-tree.com/literacy** to download this page.

Power Tool	Clueless	Heard of It	Know It	Could Teach It
Comprehension Reflection Prompts				
Think-Aloud for Comprehension				
Reading With Purpose				
Reciprocal Teaching				
Scavenger Hunt				
Passage Prediction				
Anticipation Guide				
Reading Aloud Picture Books				
Interactive Notebooks				
Mind Mapping				
Marking the Text				
Marginalia				
Golden Lines				
Guided Read-Aloud				
Somebody Wanted But So				
Read and Say Something				
Even Dozen				
Save the Last Word for Me				
Foldables				
Readers' Theater				
Direct Vocabulary Instruction				
Read-Alouds				

Power Tool	Clueless	Heard of It	Know It	Could Teach It
Sustained Silent Reading				
Anticipating Words				
Teaching Word Parts				
The Frayer Model				
Concept Maps				
Concept Sorts				
List, Group, Label				
Linear Array				
Mystery Word of the Day				
ABC Graffiti				
Vocabulary Rubric				
Vocabulary Graphic Organizer				
Semantic Feature Analysis				
Teacher's Vocabulary Checklist				
Writing High Five				
Response Cards				
Interactive Note-Taking				
Three-Column Journal				
Quickwrites in Journals				
Cognitive Journal Writing				
RAFT				
Cubing				
Give One, Get One				
Exit Tickets				
Think, Write, Tear, Share				
Found Poems				

Chapter 1

Engaging the Adolescent Learner

> *Adolescents entering the adult world in the 21st century will read and write more than at any other time in human history. They will need advanced levels of literacy to perform their jobs, run their households, act as citizens, and conduct their personal lives.*
>
> —*Richard Vacca*

Visualize 20 sixth-grade math students sitting in small groups eagerly awaiting instruction. As you look around the room, you see the beginning of a wall exhibit labeled "Our Community Wall." Even though it is only the third week of school, the wall displays many samples of student-generated work. Featured on the wall are math literacy timelines, vocabulary words, foldables on the topic of "High Points and Low Points in Math," biographical poems that describe student learning styles, pictures of class teams, and many other examples of student work. Classroom norms and expectations are posted on the Class Routine Chart and the Effort T-Chart. The teacher steps to the front of the room and spends 1 minute referring to the Class Routine Chart and the Effort T-Chart to remind students of expected behaviors for safety and success. The students stand, smile at each other, and say, "I am glad you are here." As they sit down, the teacher says:

> *You are absolutely not going to believe what we are going to learn today. But before you discover what it is, I want you to get into your teams. Notice that at each team spot, there is a large piece of chart*

paper and colored markers. Those are your materials for the class period. I have team instructions on an index card, which I will give you as soon as you go to your team spot. I am so excited about today, and I am going to give you a clue! As you walk to your team spot, I want you to see how many predictions you can make as to what we are going to learn.

She gives the clue and says, "One, two, three, GO!" Students move quickly to their team's spot, talking in excited tones and making predictions.

Does this sound like fiction? Well, it's not. You have just peeked inside Emerlina Binuya's sixth-grade math class in Petersburg, Virginia. What can we learn from Emerlina's class? She understands that building high student engagement begins with getting to know the learner, and her classroom community wall displays data about her students. She engages students by planning tasks that promote small group collaboration and relevant choices because she realizes adolescents want social interaction and need some control in their world.

This chapter will present strategies for getting to know adolescents and includes strategies for providing specific feedback and increasing student effort. Multiple organizational structures for small group work are featured.

Suggested Resources

Bellanca, J., & Fogarty, R. (2003). *Blueprints for achievement in the cooperative learning classroom.* Glenview, IL: Pearson Education.

Feinstein, S. (2004). *Secrets of the teenage brain.* San Diego: The Brain Store.

Ivey, G., & Fisher, D. (2005). *Creating literacy rich schools for adolescents.* Alexandria, VA: Association for Supervision and Curriculum Development.

Jensen, E. (2003). *Tools for engagement.* Thousand Oaks, CA: Corwin.

Philp, R. (2007). *Engaging tweens and teens.* Thousand Oaks, CA: Corwin.

Rutherford, P. (2002). *Instruction for all students.* Alexandria, VA: Just ASK Publications.

Sylwester, R. (2007). *The adolescent brain.* Thousand Oaks, CA: Corwin.

Did You Know?

- ◆ Engaging in reading can help close the gap for students from families of high poverty and low educational background (Guthrie, Schafer, & Huang, 2001).

- ◆ When teachers know how to model and support literacy in their subject areas, they create an environment conducive to helping students achieve fluency.

- ◆ Adolescents deserve classrooms that feel like communities, where teachers demonstrate daily that they care and want to know more about them.

- ◆ Reinforcing effort and providing feedback influence students' attitudes and beliefs.

- ◆ Students should be encouraged to personalize the instructional goals.

- ◆ Students should receive feedback that provides them with an explanation of what they are doing that is right and wrong and what they need to do to improve their work.

- ◆ Students can effectively provide some of their own feedback.

- ◆ Learning is social, and cooperative learning nurtures adolescent motivation and engagement.

Student Learning Survey

What is a Student Learning Survey?

This Student Learning Survey is a tool for teachers and students to learn more about learning preferences and interests (Tomlinson, 2003).

Why use a Student Learning Survey?

This survey is a tool for teachers to get to know students and is a reflection tool for students to assess their preferences. It also enables students to learn about each other and to begin to discuss how people are different and how they are alike. It opens up discussions about acceptance and learning to relate to each other well.

How do I use a Student Learning Survey?

1. Reproduce a copy of the Student Learning Survey for each student. Make an enlarged text copy or a PowerPoint slide to use as a model with the class.

2. Say to the students:

   Look at the first column labeled "Characteristics." As you read down the list, put a check in the second column labeled "Like Me" if the words describe you. Put a check in "Not Like Me!" if the words don't describe you.

3. Demonstrate using yourself as the example on the enlarged copy at the front of the room. Check with the students to be sure they understand the directions.

4. When the students have completed the checklist, say:

   At the bottom of your checklist is a space for you to write a summary that describes you. Be sure you reread the column that says "Like Me!" and use the information there to write your summary.

5. Put students in groups of four, and ask them to share their summary of themselves.

6. Collect all the checklists and summaries, and create a classroom book called *Extra, Extra, Read All About Us!*

Student Learning Survey

Characteristics	Like Me!	Not Like Me!
Enjoy telling stories		
Prefer gym class and sports		
Need to move; can't sit still		
Read books just for fun		
Like choices on how to do things		
Need quiet when I work		
Prefer to do writing and research		
Prefer to build or make things		
Like details		
Enjoy math class		
Like to sing or play instrument		
Prefer working in groups		
Like to plan things		
Good at planning		
Need noise when I work		
Prefer to create charts, graphs		
Prefer organizing projects		
Need to know the big picture		
Enjoy drawing and creating		
Like to do one thing at a time		
Prefer working alone		
Prefer to be told how to do things		
Not great at planning		
Enjoy word games		
Prefer to draw pictures		
Like teaching others		
Like art		
Like to be the cheerleader of the group		
Like to keep my group on task		
Enjoy the role of recorder		
Like to present or perform		

3-2-1 Biography Poem

What is a 3-2-1 Biography Poem?

The Biography Poem (Abromitis, 1994) is a framework for writing about yourself so that others will learn more about you. It is a get-acquainted activity to introduce students to each other. The 3-2-1 Biography Poem provides a format to focus students on very specific criteria.

Why use a Biography Poem?

A poem is a nonthreatening way for students to write and talk about themselves. All students are encouraged to share information so that students of all socioeconomic levels and cultures are included. It is useful at the beginning of school or at the beginning of a course of study.

How do I use a Biography Poem?

1. Instruct students to respond to the prompts on the 3-2-1 Biography Poem Template. Guide students to write quickly; there are no wrong answers.

2. Tell students to use the information on the graphic organizer to write a poem about themselves in the box labeled: *It's About Me!*

3. When students complete their poems, ask them to join two other students and share poems. Ask them to notice the similarities and differences among partners.

3-2-1 Biography Poem Template

Three descriptive traits . . .	
Lover of [list 2 things] . . .	
Who learns best by [list 1 way] . . .	
Name . . .	
It's About Me! Use the information on the 3-2-1 and write a summary about yourself. Be ready to share your summary with a small group.	

People Search

What is a People Search?

People Search (Bellanca & Fogarty, 2003) is an interactive strategy for building learning communities. Students talk to each other to find someone who can respond to any of the statements on the handout. The student who can respond writes his name by the statement and moves on to fill in the other parts of the game. The activity keeps going until someone in the group has all of the statements signed. Another name for this activity is "Find Someone Who . . ."

Why use a People Search?

A People Search is a fun, nonthreatening way to find out information about students. It is a structured, active participation strategy that engages 100% of the students and encourages them to interact with each other.

Find someone who . . .	Signature
Can describe one current event reported this week	*Lisa Jones*
Checked out a book from the library this week or month	*Randall Brown*
Can summarize what we learned in the last class	*Kim Nguyen*
Can share a book they hope to read for fun this year	*Paul Alessio*
Can describe what they do when they can't understand what they are reading	*Joseph Baumgartner*
Can talk about a book they read that they really liked	*Maria Espinoza*
Can define their feelings about reading	*Ali Franks*

How do I use a People Search?

1. Design a People Search similar to the one in the following example. Create a list of a variety of statements that range from music, food, people, pets, or anything personal, to things that have to do with learning. Create anywhere from 5 to 10 statements.

2. Tell the students that when you say "Go!" they are to find students who will discuss one of the statements and sign in the corresponding box if it pertains to them. Students must find a *different* person for each statement; a person may sign an individual's sheet only one time. When one student has completed the People Search, the rest of the class sits down.

3. Finally, call on a student to share who signed his People Search next to the first item, then move quickly through the rest of the items.

Literacy History Timeline

What is a Literacy History Timeline?

This activity asks students to reflect on their literacy experiences, from early childhood to the present date, by recalling and illustrating significant memories of reading.

Why use a Literacy History Timeline?

The Literacy History Timeline provides insight for the teacher into students' experiences with literacy, both positive and otherwise, and helps to build connections among students in the classroom when timelines are shared and displayed. This is a useful activity to use for getting to know students at the beginning of a school year.

How do I use a Literacy History Timeline?

1. First, create your own timeline to share with students and to use as a model, or plan on completing the activity with them in class.

2. Distribute colored markers and large sheets of construction paper to students.

3. Direct students to think back on their first memory of reading of any kind. Ask:

   Do you remember your first encounters with reading, such as a parent or relative reading one of your favorite books or telling a story?

   Ask students for two or three examples to check for understanding.

4. Explain how to create a timeline. Be sure students know to use a horizontal layout and to start timelines on the left side of the paper. Demonstrate with your model. Guide students as follows:

   Think back to your first memory of reading. How old were you? On your timeline, you might have a section called Early Beginnings, age 2–5; your next time segment might be Elementary Years; the next time segment could be Now. Label each segment, and then list and illustrate some of the memories you have about reading or books you remember.

5. Change the introduction and questions used for math, science, and history classes to focus on first memories of literacy in those subjects. For example, ask:

   What is your first memory of reading or writing about science (or math or history)? What science books and topics have you read?

6. Give students at least 10 minutes or more to create their Literacy History Timelines.

7. Allow time for students to share, in small groups, significant events and experiences from their timelines.

Reading and Writing Interest Inventory

What is a Reading and Writing Interest Inventory?

A Reading and Writing Interest Inventory collects the literacy and learning preferences of students.

Why use a Reading and Writing Interest Inventory?

When you know the interests of your students, you can plan lessons that capitalize on them. Students are more likely to be motivated in something in which they are interested. The inventory also helps you learn about each student's experience as a learner.

How do I use a Reading and Writing Interest Inventory?

1. There are many examples of Reading and Writing Interest Inventories. Use the one on page 13, or create your own.

2. Distribute it to the students, and explain why you are asking them to respond and how you are planning to use the information. Make sure they understand the questions.

3. Collect the results and use them to plan lessons, to help students plan for assignments, and to develop a relationship with the students.

Reading and Writing Interest Inventory

(Created for Project CLASS by Gay Ivey [2006b] and used with permission.)

Reflect on your reading interests and learning preferences, and write your answers to the following questions.

If you could read anything, what would it be? Why?

What makes you want to read in (name of subject area)?

Write about a good experience you had with reading in (name of subject).

Write about a bad experience you had with reading in (name of subject).

Write about a good experience you had with writing in (name of subject).

Write about a bad experience you had with writing in (name of subject).

What kinds of reading do you do outside of school?

What are your favorite things to do outside of school?

What have teachers done that helps you the most with reading?

When have you felt really proud of yourself? Why did you feel this way?

What pushes your "hot button?" (Or, what do you hate?)

What else would you like me to know about you as a person and a student that will help me teach you better?

Class Routine Chart

What is a Class Routine Chart?

A Class Routine Chart articulates clear and explicit norms and expectations to learners so they will know what you expect and how they can contribute to a successful class.

Why use a Class Routine Chart?

A Class Routine Chart helps students perceive the classroom as a comfortable, safe, and orderly place. It can communicate how we do business within our learning community. Consistent use of rules and procedures has a positive impact on student behavior and student learning.

Sample Class Routine Chart

We start and end class on time. If you are not here, we will start without you and hold you accountable for what you missed.

We need opportunities to stretch, stand, and move while working. We will take some type of break every 20 minutes.

We will read every day.

We will write about what we are reading and learning every day.

We will use the Effort T-Chart daily. We will build a community of learners by working in pairs and small groups. We will listen to others and do our share.

We will reflect on our learning every day. We will help keep our room clean and orderly.

How do I use a Class Routine Chart?

1. Begin by planning a lesson that could feature a story, poem, or movie clip that focuses on behavior and learning.

2. Facilitate a discussion of what the class read or viewed; end with identifying the positive and negative aspects of routines.

3. Group the students in small groups and ask:

   What behaviors do we need to exhibit over the year to make sure we learn, we are safe, and we have fun?

4. Students list their ideas on index cards. Each group shares their suggestions.

5. Place the index cards on the wall.

6. Allow time for groups to share, then ask the class to select the index cards they think are most important and rewrite them to say exactly what they mean.

7. Add your ideas to the list.

8. Post the list on the wall, and refer students to it every day so that it becomes a part of the learning community culture.

The Effort T-Chart

What is the Effort T-Chart?

The Effort T-Chart is a graphic organizer that organizes information into concrete, specific, observable behaviors that demonstrate effort using two of the five senses—seeing and hearing.

Why use the Effort T-Chart?

Using this structure helps the student and the teacher to assess if the level of understanding of "effort" is vague or if there is a deep understanding of the concept. Once the students have agreed on what effort would look like and sound like, they achieve a consistent understanding of the concept as a class. This is very important, as all students must have the same understanding if it is to be the model to aspire to during the year.

How do I use the Effort T-Chart?

1. First, provide clear and compelling examples and models of effort by using stories and videos of real people—celebrities, athletes, and people your students know in the school and community. This is key because many students do not understand the concept of effort and have very little background knowledge.

2. Create a T-chart on a transparency, PowerPoint slide, chart paper, or the board. Generate a dialogue about the story, character, movie, or neighborhood person you introduced, and have the students generate a list of five or six attributes that made the person successful.

3. Write the headings *Effort Looks Like* and *Effort Sounds Like*. Take each of the words and ask the students what they would see and hear if a person was doing that word. Ask how they would know.

4. Involve several classes in discussing effort attributes to create one T-Chart that works for all classes. Students can view and discuss one group's effort chart and add ideas. This will enable use of one T-Chart for classes.

Use the T-Chart every day by:

♦ Recording student descriptions of their effort

♦ Celebrating when effort is demonstrated

♦ Selecting the "effort of the day" behavior to practice

♦ Asking students to select specific effort behaviors that are essential to use in taking tests, especially standardized tests

♦ Asking each student to select an effort behavior from the T-Chart and work on it for a week

♦ Meeting with an effort partner every Friday to discuss how well they are doing on effort

♦ Meeting with the class, once a grading period, to discuss effort and adding to the T-Chart if the students have a new attribute

♦ Reading stories about people and effort

♦ Planning an effort conference with each student once a grading period

♦ Writing in a journal about effort

♦ Displaying an effort thermometer in class: Raise the degrees when 100% of students give 100% effort on a homework assignment, group work, and so on

The Effort T-Chart

Effort Looks Like	Effort Sounds Like
♦ Doing work over and over until it is the best I can do	♦ Asking questions until I understand
♦ Spending time reviewing	♦ Making comments about effort such as, "I am tired, but I worked hard—I made a good effort."
♦ Studying together with a partner	♦ Rewriting: "This is going to be hard. I may have to re-write this more than once."
♦ Completing assignments	♦ Reading and writing notes such as, "I am really going to have to study."

Let Your Fingers Do the Walking

What is Let Your Fingers Do the Walking?

Let Your Fingers Do the Walking is a simple protocol that allows learners to quickly preview learning material by skimming through it for 3 or more minutes.

Why use Let Your Fingers Do the Walking?

Let Your Fingers Do the Walking helps introduce the topic, the textbook, or the course. It builds interest in learning the new material and has the potential of creating a state of anticipation on which the teacher can build. It assists the learner in seeing the "big picture" of the whole text. It also takes away some of the fear learners may have about a subject or topic when they look through the material and connect with prior knowledge they have.

How do I use Let Your Fingers Do the Walking?

1. Select the text or other material that will be used for the subject, course, or topic and say:

   For the next 3 minutes, look through your materials. Scan the pages, and look at titles, headings, graphics, and other features. As you browse your text, you may talk to your neighbors. For example, if you see something you think is interesting, it is okay for you to say, "Hey, this looks interesting. I remember studying a little about this last year." Your chatter must focus on the text.

2. Instruct students:

   Flag pages that spark your interest. On sticky notes, jot down page numbers and topics that you'd like to learn about, talk about, or experience.

   Browse for 3 minutes, and be ready to share your topics of interest.

3. Call on four to six students to share one page that interested them. When a student shares the page and topic, the teacher responds by first asking if any other students in the class had the same page and topic. When they are identified, the teacher builds community by saying:

   Great, look how many other students think like you do.

The teacher also responds to the topics by making comments that generate curiosity and anticipation:

That is my favorite topic. Let me tell you one thing about it that I bet you did not know.

The processing of this is very important because it is here that the teacher has the ability to generate interest or create a state of curiosity.

4. Collect the sticky notes with the page numbers and the topics to put on the Community Learning Wall (page 20).

5. Encourage students to read the Learning Wall at the beginning of class to see what other classes found interesting.

Community Learning Walls

What are Community Learning Walls?

Community Learning Walls offer an interesting, interactive way to build a learning community. Through the shared responses and exhibited student work samples, teachers learn about their students, and students learn about each other. Community Learning Walls collect student responses to a teacher prompt; they are intended to make students' thinking public (Weber, 2003). Teachers can use them to monitor progress and development toward learning goals—to recognize how the class is thinking and growing.

Why use Community Learning Walls?

Community Learning Walls showcase student work and thinking and acknowledge student effort and achievement. Learning Walls help to develop a sense of connectedness among students and teachers and send the message that this is a student-centered classroom.

Learning Walls are dialogue boards and student work exhibits on which students interact to prompts and/or each other. Use them to 1) activate prior knowledge and experience, 2) assess what students already know about a topic, 3) stimulate dialogue between students based on an opinion statement, and 4) help students reflect on their learning. Students can see how their classmates are thinking and how they respond to prompts.

Community Learning Walls collect performance data over time on individual students, groups of students, and classes. They are an easy form of assessment to administer, and teachers can quickly see who's "got it" and who needs more instructional practice. The Wall becomes another visual form of specific feedback as individuals and groups discuss what the data on the walls mean.

Learning Walls can help students make connections among essential knowledge in units of study. Displaying posters that summarize and synthesize the big ideas of each unit can serve as "teaching-learning" walls when students review and discuss the content displayed. Learning Walls offer critical support to teachers of classrooms with high mobility, absenteeism, and student turnover.

How do I construct a Community Learning Wall?

1. Use all the walls in your classroom to accommodate multiple groups or classes of students, or take a minimalist approach and make your Learning Wall from chart paper, poster board, or vacant space on a board.

2. Establish a materials and supplies corner. Fill a container with scissors, construction paper, colored markers, paper, and lots of sticky note pads of various colors.

3. Plan the topics that you will emphasize on your Learning Wall, and identify space within your classroom. Learning Walls can feature a variety of data, student responses, and sample work. Descriptions of a few types of exhibits follow.

Community Corner

Create a learning community response board to generate interest and elicit students' opinions related to a topic. Students write their ideas on sticky notes marked with their student numbers or names to record their responses. Add sticky notes to each student's file to store individual data. Secondary teachers can use color-coded sticky notes for different classes.

Data Dig

Create an area that displays and summarizes classroom data in bar graphs and other visual representations. For example, students could each write their favorite type of music on a sticky note, then create a bar graph showing the frequencies of each type of music, and discuss the results. Another data dig could elicit and summarize the topics students are most interested in learning using the data generated from Let Your Fingers Do the Walking (pages 18–19).

Learning Styles

Select a Learning Styles survey of your choice. After students have completed the inventory, create a bar graph showing the frequencies of each style, and discuss the results.

The Know Zone

Use the Frayer Model (page 116) as a framework for assessing students' background knowledge of a concept. Write the topic in the center of the square, and have students place their responses in the appropriate box before they read the selected text. After they read and learn new information, students revise their thinking by writing and posting new information on different colored sticky notes and taking away inaccurate information.

The Gallery

Exhibit student work samples that represent "blue ribbon" effort. These could be posters, reports, foldables, study guides, and other projects. Try to display every student's work during the grading period.

Goal Setting

What is Goal Setting?

Goal Setting "is the process of establishing a direction for learning. It is a skill that successful people have mastered to help them realize both short-term and long-term desires" (Marzano, Pickering, & Pollock, 2001, p. 93).

Why use Goal Setting?

Setting goals helps students to create a clear picture of what they are expected to learn. Setting and monitoring goals enables students to determine what they need to do in order to be successful, and holds them accountable. This process also inspires and motivates students to accomplish goals.

How do I use Goal Setting?

1. Before beginning a unit of study, allow time for students to preview the material using Let Your Fingers Do the Walking (pages 18–19) or another strategy that provides an overview of what is to be learned.

2. Share the objectives of the class, course, or unit, and ask students to write the objectives in their journal, binder, or interactive notebook for the unit. Students must understand the learning objectives so that they can work to achieve the desired level of performance.

3. Post goals and objectives on the walls of the classroom, and refer to them at the start of lessons. Ask students to reflect on the goals and objectives, and then to create one personal learning goal and write that goal in a journal or interactive notebook. Explain why reaching identified goals is important, and that students will be responsible for achieving goals.

4. Pair students to form Learning Goal Partners for the unit. Allow time for Learning Goal Partners to meet weekly to discuss their progress: 1) what they are doing well to accomplish their goal and 2) what they need to improve or do differently to be successful. As students take turns discussing their goals, circulate throughout the room to listen, assess, and give specific feedback.

5. Ask each student to independently write a summary of the learning goal session with his or her partner on an Exit Ticket (page 166). Read the tickets and write feedback to the Learning Goal Partners. Keep the Exit Tickets for each pair to use as an assessment for weekly progress.

Specific Feedback

What is Specific Feedback?

Sometimes it helps to define a concept by thinking about what it is not. Specific Feedback is *not* praise. It can include praise but goes beyond the familiar "Excellent! Good job!" or "Wrong." Specific Feedback is one of nine instructional strategies that work to increase student achievement (Marzano, Pickering, & Pollock, 2001) and provide students with specific information as to how well they are performing.

Why use Specific Feedback?

Specific Feedback has a powerful impact on learning and achievement and is important to help learners assess the degree to which they have accomplished goals (Marzano, Pickering, & Pollock, 2001). Feedback can be provided by the teacher, peers, and the learner.

How do I use Specific Feedback?

1. Give students feedback that tells them exactly what is correct or incorrect in their work. Tell students the correct answer and explain. For example:

    Your paragraph meets expectations because it contains a topic sentence and supporting details.

2. Give feedback as soon as possible after a task or test to impact learning. Time is important. For example, allowing partners to assess each other's work the day after a test will have more impact on learning than you as the teacher checking and handing back results a week later. It's important to know that students can participate in giving feedback to peers. However, be sure to teach students how to give and receive feedback by modeling and using checklists and rubrics that specify the criterion for assessments.

3. Try Pause, Prompt, and Praise as a structure for feedback. It provides an example for specific and corrective feedback. When a student or group of students appears to be struggling with a challenging task, take the following steps:

◆ **Pause**—Ask the student to stop working on the task. Briefly discuss why the student is struggling with this task. It might sound like this:

Henry, stop what you are doing, and let's reflect. What is it about the task that you know you understand? Now tell me what it is about the task that is confusing.

By asking both questions, the teacher is encouraging reflective thinking and gaining a better understanding of the metacognitive process of the student.

◆ **Prompt**—Provide a specific suggestion for improving the student's performance:

You are right on the mark when you told me you were trying to remember what to do when you could not understand hard reading material. You said you did not remember all the things to do, so let me remind you of one of the tools you can use. Look on our Community Learning Wall. Do you see the section titled Trouble With Text? *There are seven suggestions. I am going to ask you to use one of them for now. Look at the one that says* Asking Questions.

Review this comprehension strategy with the student, then model using a Think-Aloud with the student's reading assignment. Ask the student to do this, and to write the questions on sticky notes. Let him or her try one before you leave.

◆ **Praise**—Praise the student for his or her effort if the performance improves as a result of using the suggestion. This might sound like:

Your question is a good one. Also, in order for you to understand this material, you have to know the answer to your question. Keep reading for the answer, and also see if you can come up with at least four more questions. I look forward to seeing what your other questions are going to be because the first one was so thought-provoking. I can tell you are thinking!

◆ Leave the student to work independently, and continue to monitor the class. Circulate around the entire class, then stop again by the student's desk to see that he or she is on the right track.

Checklist for Student Self-Assessment

What is a Checklist for Student Self-Assessment?

A Checklist for Student Self-Assessment provides specific information to students on what is expected. Elements or criteria for a task are listed; this helps to guide students sequentially through each step of the process of completing an assignment (Burke, 2006).

Why use a Checklist for Student Self-Assessment?

A Checklist for Student Self-Assessment helps students achieve higher quality work because it shows them exactly what they have done or not done. It also encourages individual accountability during cooperative group work by specifying concrete behaviors expected for successful performance.

How do I use a Checklist for Student Self-Assessment?

Kay Burke suggests the following steps for creating checklists (2006):

1. Create a heading that includes the title of the assignment, the numbers of the state standards, and the focus of the standards, such as *branches of government.*

2. List the criteria or elements for assessing the final product. The criteria include the specific directions for students to follow. Use vocabulary words and synonyms from state standards. Bullet the elements that will be assessed.

3. Decide on an overall point value and scoring for the assignment that illustrates the grading scale and final grade earned. Assign one point for "Yes" or "Some Evidence." Assign zero points for "0," "No Evidence," or "Not Yet."

4. Decide on the format of the checklist and consider using graphics, space for checkmarks and comments, bold print for headings or key terms, and color.

5. Arrange the items on the checklist in correct sequence.

6. Distribute the checklist to the students when you are explaining the assignment.

7. Have students fill out the checklist, and instruct them to attach a copy to the assignment once it is completed.

Encourage student reflection and self-assessment by asking students to describe the effort they expend on assigned tasks by using checklists and rubrics. Have them give themselves an "effort rating."

Student Rubric for Grading Notebooks

Name _____ Date _____

Possible Points		Points Earned
20	Number of finished assignments (5 points for each of 4 assignments)	
1	Table of contents (1 point—Complete next section)	
1	Assignments in order (1 point)	
22	Total	
TABLE OF CONTENTS		
Assignment Number	Title of Assignment	Grade
1		
2		
3		
4		

Class Expectations Survey

Read and mark the questions or items that you need to improve on during this unit.

____ **How much time do you invest in this class?** To get a B or better, you will need to spend time *in* class listening, taking notes, and thinking, and time *out* of class doing the homework, readings, and projects.

____ **Do you prepare for class?** Stay current. If you are studying chapter 4, and we are working on chapter 6, you are going to be behind, and you will most likely stay behind!

____ **When and how do you study?** It is best to review right away. Break up your study times into short periods. Don't study when you are tired. Study in a quiet, private spot. Study by *doing.* That means working the problems and answering the questions. When you get an answer right, go back over it to see why the method you used worked.

____ **Can you explain it to others?** If possible, work problems in a group or with a partner. Explain your answers. If you can explain it to others, you *know* it!

____ **Do you cram for tests?** Don't. It will not work. Do not change your study habits because a test is coming. The most useable knowledge is already there—if you have kept up. Cramming leads to fatigue, test anxiety, and stupid mistakes.

Name _____ Date _____

Student Learning Contract

Please put your initials next to each item and your signature at the end.

___1. I acknowledge that I have read and understand the requirements and assignment dates of this class. I am responsible for keeping up to date. I will not use "I forgot" or "I didn't know it was due today" as an excuse.

___ 2. I am responsible for asking questions when I do not understand the content presented. I will not use "I didn't understand or know" as an excuse for not completing an assignment on time. It is my responsibility to bring to the teacher any questions, comments, and reactions to this course that affect my ability to learn.

___ 3. I understand that this class will use active learning and cooperative learning teaching techniques. This will require participation and involvement on my part.

___ 4. I am responsible for knowing assignment dates and deadlines and for meeting these. I understand that late work will receive less credit.

___ 5. I acknowledge that the teacher is not responsible for decisions I make about how I spend my time, such as extracurricular activities, jobs, social life, or waiting until the last minute to complete assignments. My life is my responsibility.

Signature _____   Parent signature _____

My Performance in Group Work

Reflect on your cooperative group skills and task performance. How would you rate yourself for each group-work responsibility? Circle the number that best fits your performance, add up the total, and sign this form before turning it in.

> 0 = Not Yet   2 = Meets Expectations
>
> 1 = In Progress   3 = Exceeds Expectations

Responsibilities

I participated in all tasks.	0	1	2	3
I performed my assigned role:	0	1	2	3
_____				
I helped team members.	0	1	2	3
I stayed on task and used time appropriately.	0	1	2	3
I helped to monitor my team's activities.	0	1	2	3
I supported my ideas with evidence from the text/picture.	0	1	2	3
I listened to my team members.	0	1	2	3
I encouraged everyone to contribute and talk.	0	1	2	3
I was courteous to everyone.	0	1	2	3
I did not use put-downs.	0	1	2	3

> ### Scale
> 27–30 = A   21–23 = C
>
> 24–26 = B   Below 21 = Not Yet

My total score is: _____

Something that I learned today was _____

_____

I think we could make our discussion even better the next time by _____

_____

_____

Signature _____   Date _____

Strategy 1.13

Cooperative and Partnered Learning

What are Cooperative and Partnered Learning?

Cooperative Learning is a teaching strategy in which small groups of three to five students work interactively to accomplish a learning task. Each task must include the following criteria: *positive interdependence, individual accountability, equal participation,* and *simultaneous interaction.* Partnered (or Paired) Learning has the same criteria as Cooperative Learning but uses only two students. Partnered Learning is an effective way to begin getting students to work together if they are only used to individual work. Once students have shown they can work with a variety of partners, they are ready to move into a larger group of three to five students. See the Why Partners? and Grouping Strategies Bookmarks on page 193.

Why use Cooperative and Partnered Learning?

The brain learns better in a social setting. Cooperative Learning nurtures positive peer relationships, which are important to adolescent learners. It increases academic achievement and teaches students how to work on a team, a necessary skill for the future.

How do I use Cooperative and Partnered Learning?

1. Choose a piece of essential content.

2. Select one of the following student tasks to use with your content:

   - Interview each other about assigned reading.

   - Question each other about an assigned reading.

   - Read and critique each other's work.

   - Respond to a question posed by the teacher.

   - Brainstorm ideas.

   - Solve a problem.

   - Recap a demonstration on film.

   - Develop a question to ask the teacher.

3. Select one of the Cooperative Learning or Paired Learning activities on pages 32–34 to structure your assigned task.

4. Embed your content into the Cooperative Learning activity, and plan the lesson to include the essential components: individual accountability, equal participation, positive interdependence, and simultaneous interaction.

5. Pair or form cooperative groups by using partner sign-up sheets, teacher selection, counting off 1-2-3, class ranking (pair a high-achieving student with a low-achieving student and two from the middle), random pairs, or student selection. The key is to understand the objective of the assignment and to pair students accordingly; however you choose to pair or cooperatively group students, you must have a plan for the structure.

6. Monitor pairs or groups by walking around and observing. The students should be doing all the work.

Cooperative and Partnered Learning Tools

The following strategies are useful for instruction involving pairs, trios, and small groups.

Turn to Your Partner

♦ Ask students to turn to a neighbor and ask him or her to do one of the following for 3–5 minutes:

- ♦ Make three connections from the article you just read to the world in which you live.

- ♦ List three key points from the chapter you read.

- ♦ Make as many predictions as you can as to what the reading is going to be about from the title of the story.

♦ Walk around to check on the student responses. Call on three or four pairs to share their partners' responses. This increases accountability of the students.

3-Step Interview (Kagan, 1994)

1. Form pairs randomly.

2. Pose questions such as:

What do you already know about . . . ?

What are two big ideas from the selection we just read?

What connections can you make to other texts you have read?

3. Allow time for pairs to take turns interviewing each other using the questions in Step 2. Set a time limit, and tell pairs to use good listening skills and to summarize their partners' responses because they will be using the information later.

4. Form foursomes by asking each pair of students to join another pair.

5. Each student in turn introduces his or her partner to the other pair and shares the summary they wrote in relation to what the partner said in the interview: "This is my partner, Carol, and she said that . . ."

Numbered Heads Together (Kagan, 1994)

1. Organize students in groups of four, and have students number off, 1-2-3-4. Tell them to take a sheet of paper and write at the top the number they were assigned. Ask a question such as:

We've just read about three countries in South America. Which country would your group prefer to live in, and why?

2. Have students "put their heads together" to determine one group response. They can use their selected reading to discuss or to read deeper for their group response. Once they decide on a quality response, tell them each member in the group needs to write down the group response on the paper they wrote their number on because they will be sharing it with a different group very soon.

3. Assign a number from 1 to 4 to each corner of the room. These numbers correspond to the numbers assigned to students in Step 1.

4. Direct all students with that number to go to that corner and stand with their new group. Check to be sure that the students are in the group that corresponds to the original number they wrote down and that they have their written group response ready to share.

5. Signal for each group to begin round-robin sharing of their original group's response.

6. Walk around to all groups to listen to responses.

Jigsaw Modified

1. Divide the textbook chapter or other reading material into segments. Material can be divided into two, three, or four sections. Do not use more than four segments. Make copies of each segment if needed.

2. Ask students to number off according to the number of segments. For example, if there were four segments, students would number off 1 to 4. Tell them that each group of 1 to 4 is a "Home Team"; direct students to jot down the names of their Home Team members.

3. Tell the Home Team members that they are going to be sent away from their team to become Experts on a topic. Ask all of the 1's to go to a specific spot. Give all of the 1's the *same* segment of reading material, and tell them to read it silently and underline main points. Next, they are to discuss with their Expert Team the ideas they might all use to teach this to each of their Home Teams. They are to prepare the same presentation to take back to the Home Team. They may choose to create a visual, such as a chart, or a summary of key points. The key is that the entire Expert Team prepares one visual or summary so that there will be consistency. Do the same with Expert Teams 2, 3, and 4. Each Expert Team has a different section of the text to read and prepare.

4. Ask students to return to their Home Teams to present what they have learned from their Expert Team.

5. After the students have had time to present, design an assessment of the reading to determine how well the students captured the main ideas of the different sections.

Focus Trios

1. Group students into trios.

2. Before a film, lecture, or reading, have trios summarize together what they already know about the subject and come up with two to five questions about the topic.

3. After the film, lecture, or reading, ask the trios to write the answers to questions, discuss new information, create a visual of what they learned, and formulate new questions.

Summary Pairs

Have pairs of students alternate reading and orally summarizing paragraphs; one reads and summarizes while the other checks the paragraph for accuracy and adds anything left out. They alternate roles with each paragraph. Or, have students elaborate on what they are reading and learning by relating it to what they already know about the subject. This can be done before and after reading a selection, listening to a lecture, or seeing a film.

Reflection and Application

Review the strategies in this chapter for engaging adolescent learners, and select three to five strategies that you plan to try. Begin by thinking about your existing lessons. Which strategy can you add to an existing lesson plan? You may also want to think about identifying specific standards or objectives with which you will use the strategies. Alternatively, what tool can you change or modify for your classroom?

Teacher Tools	What do I NOT want to try?	How can I add this to an existing lesson?	What different standards can I use it with?	What tool can I change or use another way?
Student Learning Survey				
3-2-1 Biography Poem				
People Search				
Literacy History Timeline				
Reading and Writing Interest Inventory				
Class Routine Chart				
The Effort T-Chart				
Let Your Fingers Do the Walking				
Community Learning Walls				
Goal Setting				
Specific Feedback				

Teacher Tools	What do I NOT want to try?	How can I add this to an existing lesson?	What different standards can I use it with?	What tool can I change or use another way?
Checklist for Student Self-Assessment				
Class Expectations Survey				
Student Learning Contract				
My Performance in Group Work				
Cooperative and Partnered Learning				
Turn to Your Partner				
3-Step Interview				
Numbered Heads Together				
Jigsaw Modified				
Focus Trios				
Summary Pairs				

Notes for lesson planning:

Chapter 2

Empowering Strategic Learning

> *The empirical evidence for single strategy instruction (Duke and Pearson, 2002) is substantial and consistent: students who learn specific strategies can apply them, resulting in increased comprehension of the texts to which they are applied and transfer to the comprehension of new passages.*
>
> *—Linda Darling-Hammond*

Elizabeth Gregory routinely begins her classes each day with a 1-minute reading in which she models fluent reading and shares an excerpt from a book or other resource that she thinks might hook students into reading. It's her own version of National Public Radio's *Moment in History.* She understands the power of reading in learning history and tries to engage her eighth-grade students in reading daily—reading the social science textbook, newspapers, primary sources, and self-selected reading materials. However, Elizabeth observes that many adolescents struggle to make sense of challenging textbooks and to engage in sustained reading of lengthy texts. She's heard other middle school teachers complain that their students lack motivation, perseverance, and skills to read, and she knows that most will often just give up and tell the students what they need to know.

Although not a reading teacher, Elizabeth accepts her responsibility to help struggling readers. She explicitly teaches the seven comprehension strategies by modeling what good readers do to make sense of difficult text. She plans single strategy lessons during which she thinks aloud while reading an excerpt from the textbook and modeling how good readers use comprehension strategies. She routinely models how to make connections between prior knowledge and what the chapter is about, because she knows that if she does not engage students' prior knowledge and experience, they fail to learn the concepts—or learn them just for the test and then forget them. Elizabeth repeatedly models making connections and the other six comprehension strategies until they become so routine that her students speak the "comprehension" language by using the names of the strategies in class discussions.

Knowing that learning is social, especially for adolescents, Elizabeth organizes collaborative groups in a routine called Reciprocal Teaching that emphasizes a set of four strategies and provides guided practice of multiple strategies while reading text. Students are accountable for assuming one of the four roles of inferring/predicting, clarifying/monitoring, questioning, and summarizing. Because she knows some students struggle to sustain attention while reading, she holds them accountable for making their thinking visible by using sticky notes to write their questions, predictions, and other notes. Reciprocal Teaching is a routine in Elizabeth's classroom that scaffolds students' comfort, confidence, and competence. She feels the pressure all teachers feel to follow district expectations and "cover" content, but she's confident that the strategies her students use every day will support them in understanding her textbook, performing well on the standardized assessments, and reading independently, beyond her classroom and the school.

The previous chapter presented instructional strategies for increasing engagement and motivation. The purpose of this chapter is to answer a frequently asked question: *What can teachers do to promote comprehension of the challenging texts students encounter in middle and high schools?* Although this is a complex question without a single, quick solution, the first steps for all content teachers are to provide 1) time for reading and 2) high-interest materials that students are able to read. Then content teachers must help students to read difficult text by teaching strategies.

This chapter describes the "Magnificent Seven," the seven comprehension strategies that all readers need to use, and explains why adolescents need to know and use these strategies. We also present explicit steps for teaching comprehension strategies and emphasize that all content teachers must model these strategies, not just English language arts teachers. You'll also find directions on how to use the instructional strategy called Reciprocal Teaching and other instructional strategies and graphic organizers that increase student engagement and comprehension before, during, and after reading.

Suggested Resources

Gregory, V., & Rozzelle, J. (2005). *The learning communities guide to improving reading instruction.* Thousand Oaks, CA: Corwin.

Harvey, S., & Goudvis, A. (2000). *Strategies that work.* Portland, ME: Stenhouse.

Robb, L. (2000). *Teaching reading in middle school.* New York: Scholastic.

Robb, L. (2003). *Teaching reading in social studies, science, and math.* New York: Scholastic.

Wilhelm, J. (2001). *Improving comprehension with think-aloud strategies.* New York: Scholastic.

Did You Know?

♦ Good readers use seven comprehension strategies: 1) making connections to prior knowledge, 2) drawing inferences, 3) asking questions, 4) determining what is important, 5) visualizing the content, 6) synthesizing and retelling, and 7) monitoring and using appropriate fix-up strategies to repair reading (Pearson, Roehler, Dole, & Duffy, 1992).

♦ Good readers use multiple strategies automatically and simultaneously: before they read to activate prior knowledge and set purpose, during reading to focus attention and interact with text, and after reading to reflect, summarize ideas, and evaluate the usefulness of the information gleaned.

♦ When teachers model, not just mention, the seven comprehension strategies, student achievement increases (Duke & Pearson, 2002).

♦ Reciprocal Teaching structures student application and practice of comprehension strategies in small group instruction and increases student performance (Palinscar & Brown, 1984.)

The Magnificent Seven Comprehension Strategies

What are the Magnificent Seven Comprehension Strategies?

Reading is the strategic thinking we do to make sense of text. It requires skill in decoding and constructing meaning and the intentional use of strategies to understand text. Good readers use seven strategies to make sense of what they read and solve problems, just as forensic scientists use strategies and tools to solve crimes. Research confirms that good readers use the following seven comprehension strategies (Pearson, Roehler, Dole, & Duffy, 1992).

1. **Making connections to prior knowledge:** Connecting the information in the text to prior knowledge and personal experiences, other texts, world events, people, or issues

2. **Inferring and predicting:** Reading between the lines to find answers to questions and draw conclusions

3. **Asking questions:** Interacting with the text and asking questions of the author, yourself, and the text

4. **Determining important ideas and summarizing:** Identifying the big ideas and themes and differentiating essential information from less important ideas

5. **Visualizing:** Creating pictures in your mind while reading, using your other senses, too—taste, hearing, touch, smell

6. **Synthesizing and retelling:** Combining the other comprehension strategies and information from different sources to produce a new idea or way of describing something

7. **Monitoring and clarifying understanding of text:** Thinking about your thinking while reading, realizing when you don't understand what you're reading, and using strategies to solve your comprehension problem

Why use the Comprehension Strategies?

Many students in the middle and upper grades are passive readers and do not know what to do when they have trouble making sense of what they read. They stare at the page, read the words, but can't tell you what they've read. All intellectual powers depend on reading. Use of these Comprehension Strategies is essential for success in school, college, and in life. Good readers use these strategies to do the following:

♦ Stay engaged rather than daydreaming while reading boring text.

♦ Understand highly technical information.

♦ Make sense of challenging textbooks.

♦ Perform successfully on standardized tests.

♦ Retain information gained from reading.

How do I use Comprehension Strategies?

Making Connections

1. Explain to the class that readers make connections between new information in text and their prior knowledge and experience; they seek connections to their own life, other texts they've read, and to the world. Good readers ask: "Does this text remind me of something I already know? What do I know about this topic?"

2. Direct students to create two columns for note-taking: *What This Is About* and *What This Reminds Me Of*. Ask them to read a selection of text, and write the important ideas in the first column and connections in the second column.

3. See Golden Lines (page 84) for a graphic organizer to promote making connections.

Inferring and Predicting

1. Explain to students that inferring is reading "between the lines." To read between the lines, readers must connect what is in the text with what they already know and make a prediction or draw a conclusion. Good readers use background knowledge to answer questions, interpret difficult text, or generate hypotheses.

2. Direct students to use a two-column graphic organizer during reading to note *Facts* and *Inferences/Predictions*.

3. Use Passage Prediction (page 69) to help students infer and predict what they will learn.

Asking Questions

1. Explain to students that readers focus better when they ask questions that 1) clarify meaning, 2) predict what will happen, 3) interact with the author's information, or 4) find a specific answer in the text.

2. Direct students to write questions on sticky notes or in the margin of the text before, during, and after reading. Say:

   Think of "thick" questions—questions that have many possible answers that you can find in different parts of the text—as well as "thin" questions that call for only one answer that you can usually find in just one place.

3. See Marking the Text (page 78) or Marginalia (page 80) for structures that help students generate questions.

Determining Important Ideas and Summarizing

1. Instruct students to scan a selection of text and read the headings and subheadings. Say:

   As you read, ask yourself questions such as: Are there some parts of the text that are more important than others? What words, sentences, ideas, or themes stood out as especially important? Why?

2. Tell students to use sticky notes to record three important ideas from the text, write a gist statement, then create a Concept Map, Mind Map, or web to chart the big ideas.

3. See Concept Maps (page 119) or Mind Mapping (page 76) to help students determine big ideas. Somebody Wanted But So (page 89) provides a structure for learning how to summarize.

Visualizing

1. Explain to students:

   To visualize means to create pictures or movies in your mind while reading—to create a Mind Map with illustrations of the important ideas.

2. Give students a selection of text, and tell them to use images to draw or sketch a picture that represents and interprets what they read.

3. Have students write an explanation for the nonlinguistic representation or drawing and share with others. They can act out the message or important ideas of the text.

4. See Golden Lines (pages 84) for a graphic organizer that promotes visualizing.

Synthesizing and Retelling

1. Explain that synthesizing means to connect different parts of the text to create an overall meaning or theme, during and after reading.

2. Give students two sources or texts on the same topic to read. Have them search for common elements and elements that are different and use a Venn Diagram to compare and contrast ideas or information.

3. Say:

   If you were to tell a friend about the text in a few sentences, what would you tell them?

4. Use Even Dozen (page 92) as a graphic organizer to help students synthesize important ideas.

Monitoring and Clarifying Understanding of Text

1. Tell students that you'd like them to think about their thinking while reading:

   Try to realize when meaning breaks down or when you "space out" during reading.

2. Explain to students that to monitor and clarify comprehension while reading the text:

   You can use "fix-up" strategies such as rereading, skipping a difficult part and reading ahead to clarify, changing your reading rate to slow down or speed up, stopping and thinking about what you already read, and thinking aloud to ask questions, predict, make a connection, or visualize what you've read.

3. Ask students to use sticky notes or Marginalia (page 80) to record places in the text where they used fix-up strategies.

Explicit Comprehension Instruction

What is Explicit Comprehension Instruction?

Teaching comprehension is a process, not a mystery. The comprehension strategies essential to understanding and learning content remain the same across grades and content areas; the only thing that changes is the difficulty of the text as students move up in grade level.

The most important step in the process of teaching strategies is modeling how good readers use comprehension strategies by thinking aloud as you read. Another important element is grounding the demonstration in enlarged excerpts from the content textbook, showing students how to think and read the content of mathematics, history, science, or literature.

As you model strategies, gradually shift the responsibility to the students to independently apply those strategies.

Why use Explicit Comprehension Instruction?

Our classroom observation data confirm what Dolores Durkin (1979) found decades ago: that teachers mention comprehension and assign questions to answer or worksheets to complete rather than show students how to use comprehension strategies. Many adolescents do not know or use comprehension strategies to make sense of what they read and give up too quickly. They need strategies in order to persevere through challenging textbooks and standardized tests. We explicitly teach comprehension strategies to *show* rather than tell students how to think while reading to construct meaning.

How do I use Explicit Comprehension Instruction?

Take the following simple steps to create a mini-lesson on comprehension strategies.

1. Choose a piece of text with three or four paragraphs from your textbook, newspaper, magazine, or another source. Choose an easy, short passage that you are confident every student can read. Your initial focus should be on teaching the strategy, not the content. Read the text thoughtfully to determine the strategy essential to comprehend the selected text. Use sticky notes to write your thoughts or what you will say to students when

you model the strategy. Enlarge the text to project for the whole class or small group.

2. Name and describe the strategy. For example, in describing the strategy "Make Connections," tell students this strategy involves:

   - Noting what the text reminds you of while reading

   - Making connections to prior knowledge and personal experiences

   - Connecting one text to another text

   - Making connections between world events, people, or issues

3. Tell when to use the strategy. If teaching "Make Connections," tell students that good readers use this strategy *before* they start reading to think about what they already know about the topic and *during* the reading to help them stay focused and make sense of what they are reading.

4. Model the strategy in action. This is a key step. After introducing the strategy, show students how to do it—how good readers actually comprehend! You must think aloud as you read and make your thinking "public" using your cues or sticky notes.

5. Analyze the process modeled. After modeling the strategy, ask students what they observed. Discuss their observations; ask students to analyze the process by telling you why they think you did the lesson the way you did.

6. Provide time for collaborative application. Pair students to practice the strategy with another easy piece of text that you have duplicated for this purpose. Allow time for partner students to read and prepare to share their thinking orally with partners.

7. Allow time for guided practice. Have each student practice the strategy using sticky notes so that you can observe his or her use of the strategy.

8. Promote independent practice. When assigning reading or during sustained silent reading, remind students to focus on a "strategy of the day" and use sticky notes so that you can observe their thinking.

9. Apply the strategy with increasingly difficult texts. After students learn the strategy using easy reading material, assign selections in their textbooks to apply the strategy.

Comprehension Bookmarks

What are Comprehension Bookmarks?

Comprehension Bookmarks serve as resources and scaffolds for teachers and students that define and describe what each comprehension strategy is and provide teaching and learning tips (Macomb Regional Literacy Training Center, 2003). See the Comprehension Bookmarks in the appendix (pages 185–193) for descriptions, purpose, when to use, and other tips on each strategy.

Why use Comprehension Bookmarks?

The bookmarks provide concrete support for students and teachers as they learn how and when to apply the comprehension strategies. Bookmarks include cues for using the different comprehension strategies before, during, and after reading.

How do I use the Comprehension Bookmarks?

1. Duplicate a class set of the bookmarks, and laminate for use by multiple classes, or create your own bookmarks that provide cues, sample questions, and other tips for students to use and think about while reading.

2. Enlarge the bookmarks to create classroom posters, post them on the Community Learning Wall (page 21), and remind students to use the strategies when they have trouble understanding difficult text or when writing a reflection.

3. Create sets of the bookmarks for small groups as they engage in reciprocal teaching and practice the strategies.

4. Explain to the students that they will use the bookmarks for a variety of tasks.

    ♦   Use the bookmarks in Reciprocal Teaching (page 56).

    ♦   Distribute a K-W-L chart, and ask students to discuss with a partner what they Know, what they Want to know, and what they Learned about each of the seven comprehension strategies.

    ♦   Direct students to partner and review the seven bookmarks. Together, they will select one comprehension strategy and prepare a lesson to teach to another pair of students.

♦ Select one of the bookmarks for students to take home and teach someone in their homes.

♦ Ask a student to select the comprehension strategy of the day. Encourage the students to use that comprehension strategy all period when applicable.

Comprehension Reflection Prompts

What are Comprehension Reflection Prompts?

A Comprehension Reflection Prompt is a graphic organizer that focuses on the seven comprehension strategies. The writing prompts give students an opportunity to reflect on the impact the comprehension strategies have on their ability to understand text.

Why use Comprehension Reflection Prompts?

The prompts enable the teacher to assess how the students are using the comprehension strategies, which ones have been the most helpful, and which ones need more practice or need to be retaught. The prompts help the students to see if the strategies are making a difference in their comprehension. If they are, it is hoped that the students will be more motivated to use them when they are having difficulty reading the text.

How do I use Comprehension Reflection Prompts?

1. During the first grading period, explicitly teach all seven of the comprehension strategies as described earlier in this chapter. After teaching each strategy, facilitate guided practice as students practice using the strategy demonstrated. Allow time for the students to practice, first with a partner, then independently. Teach a new comprehension strategy when observations and informal assessments indicate that the majority of the students understand the strategy. For example, on Monday, present the comprehension strategy of visualizing. Pair the students, give them a piece of text to read together, and facilitate an activity such as Golden Lines (page 84) to give students practice visualizing. Then give each student a piece of text, and ask him or her to use Golden Lines on the text individually. Use this as an assessment for deciding whether to move on to a new comprehension strategy.

2. Once students have been taught the seven comprehension strategies and have completed guided and independent practice on all of them, each student completes the Comprehension Reflection Prompt. Analyze this data to determine which comprehension strategies the students find most helpful and which need more practice.

3. Once the students learn to use all seven of the comprehension strategies, use them when assigning reading and to process all of the course content. For example, when the students are assigned reading in the text, give out sticky notes and tell the students that as they read, they are to jot down questions and make connections to other texts. Decide which of the seven comprehension strategies the students will use. The key here is that once the students learn and use all the strategies, you need to use them on a daily basis so that the students use them automatically.

4. Use this writing activity as a way of getting students to reflect on what makes a good reader.

> *As you think about yourself as a reader, reflect in writing about the following.*
>
> You have learned seven strategies to help you read. Use the comprehension strategy poster or bookmarks, and select the strategy that helps you most.
>
> What strategies help you make sense of your text?
>
> How do the seven comprehension strategies make you a better reader?
>
> Which of the seven comprehension strategies do you need more practice using?

Think-Aloud for Comprehension

What is a Think-Aloud?

A Think-Aloud (Whimbey & Whimbey, 1975) is the process of reading aloud and verbally describing steps used to think and question as we make meaning from oral, written, or visual text. It is orally describing the thinking going on inside the reader's head to make sense of the text. Think-Alouds make the reader's thinking visible, when combined with writing the thinking in the margins of the text. Over time, this mental rehearsal (the steps we say aloud) becomes a natural part of our "inner voice" for thinking.

Why use Think-Alouds?

Think-Alouds make thinking "visible" and provide models of how to use comprehension strategies. Think-Alouds model what good readers do to comprehend and make sense of text. When students do a Think-Aloud, it gives them opportunities to practice and reflect on the comprehension strategies, and it provides the teacher with insight into the student's use of strategies. Listening to students think aloud provides an assessment and information on what students need and informs strategy lesson planning.

How do I use Think-Alouds?

1. Use Think-Alouds in a variety of formats such as teacher modeling, guided practice, large or small groups with teacher and peer monitoring, or independent work with self-monitoring. A Think-Aloud is a great way to begin class every day. It shows students a technique they can use, reinforces the comprehension strategies, and models fluency.

2. Select a short piece of text for the Think-Aloud; three or four paragraphs. If using thinking aloud to model to the whole class, prepare ahead of time by reading through the text and jotting down the comments to make based on the comprehension strategy to be modeled. Project the enlarged text so the students can follow along.

3. Explain to the students what a Think-Aloud is and why it is important for them to listen.

4. Read a small part of the passage, pause, and model thinking by inserting comments from notes. To make this more concrete for students, write in the margins of the enlarged text.

   Other ways to make thinking aloud concrete for students include reading aloud a paragraph, then taking a big metaphorical action step to indicate that you are moving from reading to thinking aloud. We've seen teachers put on a baseball cap as a thinking cap, to show the transition between reading and thinking aloud.

5. After the Think-Aloud demonstration, engage the class in a discussion to analyze the process of thinking aloud, and encourage the students to ask questions about the process.

6. After modeling Think-Alouds a number of times, give the students a piece of text, teach them how to prepare a Think-Aloud, and have them practice with a partner.

Sample Think-Aloud Using a Short Article

This example is based on "Listening and Learning" (University of Washington, 2007).

First paragraph: "Researchers have found that 18-month toddlers engage in what they call 'emotional eavesdropping.'"

Think-Aloud focus: Inference—What is emotional eavesdropping? Is that like listening to a conversation when no one knows you're listening? I'm inferring that toddlers must watch and understand others' emotions.

Second paragraph: "[The toddlers listen and watch] emotional reactions directed by one adult to another and then [use] this emotional information to shape their own behavior."

Third paragraph: "Betty Repacholi and Andrew Meltzoff of the [University of Washington] Institute for Learning and Brain Sciences say the research indicates infants understand other people's emotional states at a very young age."

Think-Aloud focus: Important ideas—It seems that the big idea here is toddlers comprehend emotions of others and may imitate that behavior in another setting. They mimic reactions.

Think-Aloud focus: Generating questions—I wonder at what age babies start understanding emotions? Could it be earlier than 18 months? I wonder how researchers tested this? How did they study this behavior?

Fourth paragraph: "'The fascinating result of this study is how sensitive toddlers are to the emotional dynamics of the interactions around them. They don't need to try out a behavior of their own and get rewarded or punished, they can watch what an older brother or sister does and learn from what happens to them,' said Meltzoff, who is co-director of the Institute."

Think-Aloud focus: Summarizing—Toddlers are surprisingly sensitive to others' behaviors and emotions and learn from watching others what will be rewarded or punished.

Think-Aloud focus: Making connections—As older brothers and sisters, we should be aware that we are models for our toddler siblings.

Reading With Purpose

What is Reading With Purpose?

Reading With Purpose is a strategy for specifying what students are expected to focus on while reading and is a fundamental comprehension strategy that is essential for making connections. The teacher models reading for a purpose and provides guided practice. Eventually, students are expected to set their purpose independently.

Why use Reading With Purpose?

Reading With Purpose may be the most important strategy for promoting comprehension as well as fluency. Setting a purpose helps students to focus, connect prior knowledge with the new topic, and make sense of the reading, thus increasing comprehension.

How do I use Reading With Purpose?

1. Ask students to read the following passage, or select a piece of text that all students can read but that is challenging.

    With hocked gems financing him, our hero bravely defied all scornful laughter that tried to prevent his scheme. "Your eyes deceived" he had said. "An egg not a table correctly typifies this unexplored planet." Now three sturdy sisters sought proof. Forging along sometimes through calm vastness, yet more often over turbulent peaks and valleys. Days became weeks as many doubters spread fearful rumors about the edge. At least from somewhere, welcomed winged creatures appeared signifying momentous success. (Dooling & Lachman, 1971)

2. Tell students to read the text to figure out the meaning.

3. Call "Time!" and ask students to rate their understanding or comprehension on a scale of one to five. Ask students what the passage means, or ask them to give it a title.

4. Tell students they will read the passage again, but this time give them a title such as "Christopher Sails to the Americas." Clearly state the purpose: what you want students to read to find out.

5. Call "Time!" and ask students to rate their comprehension again as related to the purpose set for reading. Discuss why they were more successful when reading for a purpose.

6. Model reading for a purpose by reading a passage of the text and thinking aloud if the information is important or connects to the purpose.

7. Ask students to practice on another selection of text using highlighters, sticky notes, or journals.

Sample Student Instructions

1. Read "The House," and use a pen or pencil to circle whatever you think is important.

2. Read the piece again, and this time use a yellow highlighter to mark places in the text that a robber would find important.

3. Read the story a third time, and mark specific places in the story that a prospective homebuyer might think are important with a different color highlighter.

4. Contrast the three times you read and marked text. What was easier? Harder? Why?

5. On a piece of paper, make a list of what the robber would find important. Make a list of what the prospective homebuyer would find important. Compare the two lists, and discuss with a partner why each item is important. If an item is on both lists, tell why both a robber and a prospective homebuyer would find it important.

The House
(Pichert & Anderson, 1977)

The two boys ran until they came to the driveway. "See, I told you today was good for skipping school," said Mark. "Mom is never home on Thursday," he added. Tall hedges hid the house from the road so the pair strolled across the finely landscaped yard. "I never knew your place was so big," said

(continued)

Pete. "Yeah, but it's nicer now than it used to be since Dad had the new stone siding put on and added a fireplace."

There were front and back doors and a side door which led to the garage which was empty except for three parked 10-speed bikes. They went to the side door, Mark explaining that it was always open in case his younger sister got home earlier than their mother.

Pete wanted to see the house so Mark started with the living room. It, like the rest of the downstairs, was newly painted. Mark turned on the stereo, the noise of which worried Pete. "Don't worry, the nearest house is a quarter mile away," Mark shouted. Pete felt more comfortable observing that no houses could be seen in any direction beyond the huge yard.

The dining room, with all the china, silver, and cut glass, was no place to play so the boys moved into the kitchen where they made sandwiches. Mark said they wouldn't go to the basement because it had been damp and musty since the new plumbing had been installed.

"This is where Dad keeps his famous paintings and his coin collection," Mark said as they peered into the den. Mark bragged that he could get spending money whenever he needed it since he'd discovered that his Dad kept a lot in the desk drawer.

There were three upstairs bedrooms. Mark showed Pete his mother's closet which was filled with furs and the locked box which held her jewels. His sister's room was uninteresting except for the color TV which Mark carried to his room. Mark bragged that the bathroom in the hall was his since one had been added to his sister's room for their use. The big highlight in his room, though, was a leak in the ceiling where the old roof had finally rotted.

Reciprocal Teaching

What is Reciprocal Teaching?

Reciprocal Teaching (Palinscar & Brown, 1984) is a framework for talking about text or books, facilitated by the teacher and students or by small cooperative groups. The dialogue is structured by the use of four comprehension strategies: 1) summarizing, 2) question generating, 3) clarifying, and 4) predicting. The teacher and students take turns assuming the role of teacher in leading this dialogue. Visual text such as select art and photographs that align with your content area can be used to promote visual literacy.

Why use Reciprocal Teaching?

No Child Left Behind recommends Reciprocal Teaching (RT) as a research-based approach for promoting student-directed learning. RT aids students in applying and practicing comprehension strategies (summarizing ideas, asking questions, clarifying ideas and vocabulary, and predicting/inferring), improves oral language and discussion skills, and increases active student engagement. The use of photographs and art presents a "level playing field" for learning and practicing comprehension strategies, because all students regardless of reading ability can respond to a picture.

How do I use Reciprocal Teaching?

Choose text selections carefully to be certain that they lend themselves to all four comprehension strategies used in Reciprocal Teaching. Before students can use RT successfully, they need to have been taught and had time to practice those four strategies. As with cooperative learning, students need to see roles and behaviors modeled before they are assigned roles. You may vary how you use Reciprocal Teaching based on three elements: 1) what works best for your teaching style, 2) the format of the selected text, and/or 3) the learning styles of your students. Alternative approaches are described in the following sections.

1. Choose a text to model the RT roles, and enlarge the text for a whole-class demonstration lesson. As in a Think-Aloud, pre-read the text to identify segments to model the four comprehension strategies, marking or using sticky notes to note places that show prediction, clarification, question, and summary. Give students a four-column graphic organizer, or ask students to draw a four-column chart with column headings for the four different comprehension strategies.

2. Model Reciprocal Teaching by reading aloud the title of the text and any headings on the first page; make a prediction of what the text will be about. Ask students to write their prediction in the *Prediction* column. Read the first page of text, and continue as follows:

    Does anyone need to have anything clarified?

    Does anyone have a question to ask?

    My summary of what we have read is . . .

3. Discuss any clarifications, questions, and summaries, allowing time for students to record these on their graphic organizer.

4. Continue guided practice over several additional pages until students are ready to use RT independently.

5. Put students in groups of four.

6. Distribute a card to each member of the group identifying each person's unique role. Use the role cards on page 59, or create your own.

7. Have students read a few paragraphs of the assigned text selection. Encourage them to use sticky notes or their journal to help them better prepare for their roles in the discussion.

8. At the given stopping point, the **Summarizer** will highlight the key ideas up to that point in the reading.

9. The **Interrogator** will then pose questions about the selection.

10. The **Clarifier** will address confusing parts and attempt to answer the questions that were just posed.

11. The **Predictor** can offer guesses about what the author will tell the group next, or, if it is a literary selection, the Predictor might suggest what the next events in the story will be.

12. The roles in the group then switch one person to the right, and the next selection is read. Students repeat the process using their new roles. This continues until students have read the entire selection.

13. As students become more proficient with the routine, vary the roles within the group. Give out task cards with different strategies written on them; such as Quick Draw, Connector, or Big Idea). The student who has a particular card responds to the text in the manner stated on the card. See Alternative Role Cards on page 60.

Reciprocal Teaching Role Cards

Predictor

Predict what's on the next page.

- Say to your group: "I think this page is going to be about . . ."

- Use the whole page: Headings, pictures, what you already know

- Make a prediction.

- Support your prediction with evidence from the page.

- Tell your group to read the page silently.

Interrogator

Ask questions.

- Ask your group: "What is the author trying to say?"

- "What if . . ."

- "I wonder why . . ."

- "What might have happened before this?"

- "What might happen next?"

Clarifier

Clarify important ideas and words after everyone has finished reading.

- Ask your group: "Is there anything anyone does not understand?"

- "Does anyone need clarification about what we read? About the meaning of a word?"

- "Does this make sense?"

- "What evidence in the text supports our earlier prediction that . . . ? Confirm or revise our prediction with evidence."

Summarizer

Summarize information on the page.

- Tell your group what the main ideas are on the page.

- Select one big idea that you connect with or relate to.

- Say: "I think this page is about . . ."

Alternative Role Cards

Connector

Make connections to personal experiences.

- Link to other sources (visuals/texts).
- Connect to family, friends, community, and world.
- Say: "This reminds me of . . ."
- "This is different from . . ."
- "This made me remember when . . ."

VIP

Identify the big idea.

- Say: "The big idea is . . ."
- "This is important because . . ."
- "So what . . ."
- "I can use this information to . . ."
- "What title would fit this selection?"

Interrogator

Ask questions.

- Ask: "What is the author/artist trying to say?"
- "What if . . ."
- "I wonder why . . ."
- "What might have happened before this?"
- "What might happen next?"
- "Does this make sense? Why, why not?"

Quickdraw

Infer with visual images.

- Use your senses (taste, hear, feel, smell).
- Draw a picture.
- Generate mental images.
- Create a Mind Map.

Reflection and Application

Review the strategies in this chapter for empowering strategic learning, and select three to five strategies that you plan to try. Begin by thinking about your existing lessons. Which comprehension strategy can you model in an existing lesson plan? You may also want to think about identifying specific standards or objectives with which you will use the strategies. Alternatively, what tool can you change or modify for your classroom?

Teacher Tools	What do I NOT want to try?	How can I add this to an existing lesson?	What different standards can I use it with?	What tool can I change or use another way?
The Magnificent Seven Comprehension Strategies				
Explicit Comprehension Instruction				
Comprehension Bookmarks				
Comprehension Reflection Prompts				
Think-Aloud for Comprehension				
Reading With Purpose				
Reciprocal Teaching				

Notes for lesson planning:

Chapter 3

Building Comprehension

> *To read without reflecting is like eating without digesting.*
>
> *—Edmund Burke*

Ms. Hammond and Ms. Kersey are collaborative teachers in a seventh-grade inclusion classroom at Rogersville Middle School in Tennessee. They religiously model and coach their students on using the comprehension strategies, and they plan their lessons to identify and include thinking strategies before, during, and after reading. These teachers know they must ask students to use graphic organizers in order to maintain focus on and comprehension of challenging text. They often begin a unit of study by reading aloud a picture book that connects to their topic because these materials are motivating and efficient in use of time. To initiate the unit on the Civil Rights Movement, Ms. Kersey uses the Frayer Model to assess students' knowledge and experience on segregation. She uses an enlarged graphic organizer on the whiteboard to record student responses of words they associate with segregation and examples of what segregation is and is not.

Ms. Hammond models fluency and reads aloud the book *Teammates* (Golenbock, 1990), an illustrated story book by Peter Golenbock that is highly motivating and easy for all students. As she reads the story aloud, her students use their favorite guided reading graphic organizer to predict, determine the big ideas, make inferences, ask questions, visualize, and summarize. As she reads aloud, Ms. Hammond shows the illustrations and stops at preselected passages to ask students to apply comprehension strategies and write on the graphic organizer to make their thinking public or visible. She monitors to see that all students remain engaged and writing on the guided reading graphic organizer during the read aloud.

After the read aloud, Ms. Kersey asks the students to reflect on what they learned and to think of additional words and examples to add to the Frayer chart; she records their responses. Then Ms. Kersey models how to write a summary using the graphic organizer Somebody Wanted But So. She asks students to work with a partner to create a summary of *Teammates*. She gives all students an Exit Ticket and asks them to draft a description of what segregation is for the next day's class homework.

In the previous chapter, we urged teachers to model the seven comprehension strategies using Think-Alouds and textbook excerpts. In this chapter, we present a toolkit of instructional strategies and graphic organizers that emphasize use of the seven comprehension strategies. The important thing is that teams of teachers identify strategies that work for them and their students and implement those strategies across the content and across the grades so that these selected instructional strategies become routine for students. Many of the instructional strategies may be used in more than one phase of reading, but we organize them for convenience in three sections for use before, during, and after reading. Enjoy!

Suggested Resources

Allen, J. (2004). *Tools for teaching content literacy.* Portland, ME: Stenhouse.

Black, A., & Stave, A. (2007). *A comprehensive guide to readers' theatre.* Newark, DE: International Reading Association.

Flynn, R. (2007). *Dramatizing the content with curriculum-based readers theatre, grades 6–12.* Newark, DE: International Reading Association.

Robb, L. (2000). *Teaching reading in middle school.* New York: Scholastic.

Robb, L. (2003). *Teaching reading in social studies, science, and math.* New York: Scholastic.

www.rosalindflynn.com

Did You Know?

♦ Teachers increase learning when they know what students are thinking and when they connect students' prior knowledge to new information (Bransford, Brown, & Cocking, 1999).

♦ Teachers can build a high-performing community of readers when they engage adolescents with thinking tools before, during, and after reading (Daniels & Zemelman, 2004).

♦ Oral and choral reading improve fluency.

♦ Oral reading fluency needs to be included across the curriculum because of the differences in textual demands.

BEFORE READING STRATEGIES

Strategy 3.1
_____

Scavenger Hunt

What is Scavenger Hunt?

Scavenger Hunt is a tool for previewing a textbook or book; it includes a protocol of questions that guide the students' search for the contents of the book.

Why use Scavenger Hunt?

Use Scavenger Hunt to 1) give students an overview of the material so they can develop a "big picture" of the contents and 2) teach students that various features of the text contain important information. Students often ignore text features, and their comprehension suffers as a result.

How do I use Scavenger Hunt?

1. Use this instructional strategy at the beginning of the school year to introduce your textbook or when you introduce a text. You can adapt the questions for use with newspapers and other materials.

2. This works best when you select and duplicate a short chapter or part of a chapter—about five or six pages—that contains a variety of text features such as illustrations, graphs, charts, maps, and so on. Make a set for each group of five students.

3. Model how to do a Scavenger Hunt on the first page or two. Tape the pages together and post so all students can see. Use different colored markers to identify different text features:

    ♦ Circle the headings with one color, and rephrase each one into a question. Make a prediction about what information may be under the heading.

    ♦ Circle the introduction with a second color, read the first sentence, and make connections stating or writing what you already know about this in the margin.

    ♦ Circle the illustrations and/or other graphics with a third color, and read the captions and titles of the graphics aloud. Predict why this graphic is included.

- ◆ Circle the end-of-chapter questions with a fourth color, and underline key words and concepts that might tell us what is important to learn.

- ◆ Circle or highlight key vocabulary words in bold print with a fifth color, and tell what you already know about each word.

- ◆ Circle the summary with another color, and read to identify important information.

4. After modeling one or two pages, provide time for guided practice in small groups of five. Create a handout of questions for small group work, or present the following questions on enlarged text to guide the whole class in previewing the textbook. Students write responses. Duplicate the Scavenger Hunt Graphic Organizer Questions on page 68 for partners or small groups.

5. After students complete the Scavenger Hunt, prepare an informal assessment such as the Even Dozen (page 92) to check for understanding.

6. When introducing a new chapter, take the first 3 minutes of class to do a quick review of how the text is set up. Give students the message that knowing how to access the text and paying attention to different text features are very important to comprehending the material.

Scavenger Hunt Graphic Organizer Questions

1.   What is the title of the book, chapter, or article?

2.   What do you already know about this topic?

3.   What do you learn about the book from the cover?

4.   What do you predict you will learn?

5.   Examine the table of contents:

     ◆   How many units of study are presented?

     ◆   How many chapters are in the book?

6.   Circle the headings with one color, and rephrase each one into a question. Make a prediction about what information may be under the heading.

7.   Circle the introduction with a second color, read the first sentence, and make connections, stating them aloud or writing what you already know about this in the margin.

8.   Circle the illustrations and/or other graphics with a third color, and read the captions and titles of the graphics aloud. Predict why this graphic is included.

9.   Circle the end-of-chapter questions with a fourth color, and underline key words and concepts that might tell us what is important to learn.

10. Circle or highlight key vocabulary words in bold print with a fifth color, and tell what you already know about each word.

11. Circle the summary with another color, and read to identify important information.

12. Read the introduction and identify the sentences that you think are most important.

13. What kind of information is in the appendix?

14. Where are the glossary and index? What type of information is presented in each? Give an example of how each works.

Passage Prediction

What is Passage Prediction?

This strategy challenges students to sort key vocabulary words from a textbook, article, or other text into categories, and then predict what they will read in the passage based on these words (Robb, 2003).

Why use Passage Prediction?

This strategy activates and enlarges prior knowledge of vocabulary words and concepts before reading a selection. It sets a purpose for reading, creates a sense of anticipation, and actively engages students in constructing meaning before and during reading.

How do I use Passage Prediction?

1. Select a passage for the students to read, and identify 10–20 important words or phrases from the text that are associated with the major concept of the lesson.

2. Give students the title of the text and the list of words and phrases from the text. Introduce the words by pronouncing and briefly discussing the words or phrases to make sure all students are familiar with the words.

3. Organize students in pairs or small groups, and ask them to think about what the text could be about.

4. Students sort the words on the list according to which labels they think the words fit most appropriately. For example, in English class, the labels could be: *characters, problem,* or *outcome*. The rule for sorting words is that a word may be used only once.

5. Then, students use the words to write a "gist" statement that depicts a possible scenario or gist of the text. Students share their predictions before reading the text.

6. Another variation for content areas is to omit the grouping of words and ask students to write a prediction statement that describes what they will read in the text.

7. Students read the text to test their predictions and then discuss the actual gist of the story and their predictions.

Anticipation Guide

What is an Anticipation Guide?

An Anticipation Guide is a pre-reading strategy used to prepare the reader for a text and to activate prior knowledge (Daniels & Zemelman, 2004). It creates a sense of anticipation by helping the reader connect background knowledge to new content. It is simply a set of three to five statements pulled from the text; students read each statement, decide whether they agree or disagree with each statement, and write a response. You may also use three to five questions.

Why use an Anticipation Guide?

An Anticipation Guide helps students to activate and assess their prior knowledge and set a purpose for reading. It introduces key ideas or major themes that run throughout the text. Anticipation Guides provide structure for re-reading and supporting conclusions. They are useful when reading controversial text or texts with opposing perspectives.

How do I use an Anticipation Guide?

1. Read the text and identify the major concept(s) of the text or lesson, and create or pull statements from the text or questions that will challenge what readers know or believe.

2. Introduce the Anticipation Guide, and ask students to read each one of the following statements and write whether they agree or disagree with each one.

3. Ask students to write the reasons for their position on each statement in the boxes.

4. Ask students to read the text and use the form to take notes.

5. After reading, ask the students to return to the form and respond to the column on the left by marking their positions and their reasons for agreeing or disagreeing.

6. Facilitate a class discussion, and compare the before and after responses.

7. As closure, ask the students to write a summary of what they learned from the reading and the discussion.

Sample Anticipation Guide

Anticipation Guide: It's Your Life. Take Charge!

Read each one of the following statements, and write whether you agree or disagree with each one.

Before Reading	Statement		After Reading
Agree/Disagree	1. Most jobs that require low skill levels will not be needed in the workforce of the future.		Agree/Disagree
Why?		Why?	
Agree/Disagree	2. Your high school years are the most critical period of your career life.		Agree/Disagree
Why?		Why?	
Agree/Disagree	3. Dropping out of high school leads to poverty.		Agree/Disagree
Why?		Why?	
Agree/Disagree	4. Individual student effort does not improve your grades.		Agree/Disagree
Why?		Why?	
Agree/Disagree	5. The more education you have, the more money you will make.		Agree/Disagree
Why?		Why?	
Agree/Disagree	6. Math skills can help you make more money in your career.		Agree/Disagree
Why?		Why?	

Anticipation Guide Template

Fill in the statements, then write your responses.

Before Reading	Statement	After Reading
Agree/Disagree	1.	Agree/Disagree
Why?	Why?	
Agree/Disagree	2.	Agree/Disagree
Why?	Why?	
Agree/Disagree	3.	Agree/Disagree
Why?	Why?	
Agree/Disagree	4.	Agree/Disagree
Why?	Why?	

Strategy 3.4
_____

Reading Aloud Picture Books

What is Reading Aloud Picture Books?

Picture books are books that have very little print, are visually rich, and connect to concepts that are being taught. Many picture books are written on sophisticated themes such as segregation and are better suited for middle and high school grades than for elementary students.

Why use Reading Aloud Picture Books?

A picture is worth a thousand words. Students relate to visual stimuli, and all levels of readers can read a picture book. Picture books provide a brief and efficient source of reading material and are highly effective in introducing units and as models for writing.

How do I use Reading Aloud Picture Books?

1. Select the unit or the big idea that you are going to teach.

2. Find a picture book that connects in some way to the unit or big idea.

3. Read the book aloud to the class, and have them do a Guided Read-Aloud activity such as the one on page 86.

For example, *Teammates* (Golenbock, 1990) is the story of the relationship between Jackie Robinson and Pee Wee Reese. The book is rich with examples of unfair treatment, courage, friendship, taking risks, and more. If you were teaching a unit on the concept of courage, you could read the book aloud as an introductory activity and have the students talk about how the story relates to courage. See the appendix (pages 195–198) for lists of other recommended picture books.

Interactive Notebooks

What are Interactive Notebooks?

Interactive Notebooks are constructed by the student according to teacher specifications that allow the student to interact with topics, concepts, and skills being taught. There are two sides to the notebook. The right side is usually for the teacher to provide content knowledge such as readings, worksheets, vocabulary lists, and notes on the content. The left side of the notebook is for the student to interact with the content and to demonstrate learning. It might include such items as Venn diagrams comparing similarities and differences, quizzes, tests, reports, timelines, and written reflections.

Why use Interactive Notebooks?

Interactive Notebooks organize and synthesize information and serve as study guides for test preparation. They encourage the use of nonlinguistic and linguistic learning. Students of all academic and cultural backgrounds can construct them because they appeal to all learning styles. They serve as a portfolio of individual learning and help students make connections from what their teacher teaches to actual application of the information. Teachers often use them as one component in determining a grade.

How do I use Interactive Notebooks?

Distribute 11 x 17 colored construction paper. Determine if you wish for students to use all one color, follow a specific color scheme, or choose their own colors, according to your instructional purpose. Then ask students to take the following steps.

1. Create a pocketed sheet: Fold one sheet horizontally (the long way, "hotdog" style), and fit it over the long side of an unfolded sheet.

2. Fold the pocketed sheet in half to create a folder. Open the folder flat.

3. Choose another sheet for the cover, fold it in half vertically (the short way or hamburger style), and open the folded cover flat.

4. Stack the open pocketed sheet inside the opened cover.

5. Staple the pages together to make a notebook. Staple the short side of the pockets shut, and using a long-necked stapler, staple the folders to-

gether on the fold lines from the front side, leaving the staple ends inside the notebook to protect fingers.

6. Label or decorate the cover of the notebook.

7. Use gummed labels to identify the contents of each pocket.

8. Once the notebook is constructed, the teacher can use it in a variety of ways. Some classroom uses are:

    ◆ Review before a test or quiz.

    ◆ Have the students turn to a section and write a summary.

    ◆ Keep notes taken in class in the notebook.

    ◆ Have students refer to a section, join a partner, and review.

    ◆ Share with parents.

    ◆ Use as a summative assessment.

Strategy 3.6

Mind Mapping

What is Mind Mapping?

Mind Mapping is a process of using key words, symbols, graphic images, colors, and lines to show relationships among ideas (Buzan & Buzan, 2006). It is a graphic organizer that visually represents relationships among ideas, concepts, or events. Mind Mapping is a tool for organizing and retaining important information and may be used before, during, and after reading.

Why use Mind Mapping?

Mind Mapping is fun, easy to do, and useful in brainstorming ideas and organizing information. Mind Mapping can be used for taking notes, studying, and organizing and delivering a presentation. Mind Maps increase memory and retention of information. Mind Maps can be used for a quick review or to peer teach students who are absent.

How do I use Mind Mapping?

Provide whole class instruction and demonstrate how to make a Mind Map using a different colored marker for each key idea, and draw symbols or graphics to illustrate each key idea.

1. Model Mind Mapping by placing a large circle or square on the board. Write the topic in the center. Next, draw a thick line radiating from the center shape for each key idea. For example, if the topic is "Underground Railroad," some of the key lines would be *Code Words, Famous People, Dangers,* and so on. Each of those words is written in all capital letters on top of the colored lines.

2. Under each key idea, list key words that develop the idea. For example, under *Code Words,* write actual Underground Railroad code words such as *drinking gourd, quail, conductor, River Jordan,* and so on. Each word might be illustrated with a picture or a symbol to be sure it is learned in the context in which the word is used. For *drinking gourd,* the student might draw a compass to remember that *drinking gourd* was the Big Dipper, which was used to point the way north.

3. Students can use information from notes, DVDs, their text, articles, and pieces of writing to put on their Mind Maps. As students learn more information on the topic, they can add to their Mind Maps.

4. Mind Maps may be exhibited on the Community Learning Wall for students to review often.

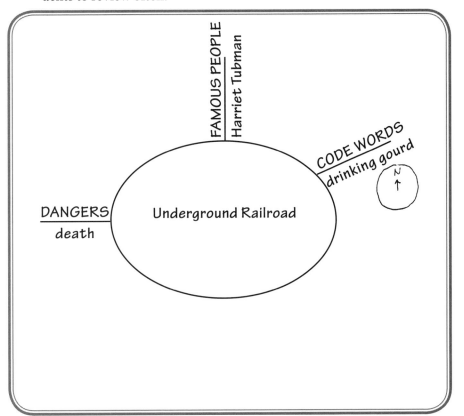

Marking the Text

What is Marking the Text?

Marking the Text is a strategy for practicing the seven comprehension strategies by using a code to represent each strategy (Davey, 1983). For example, "PK" is a code for *prior knowledge* and "VIP" can serve as the code for *very important points*. The reader marks the code in the margin as he or she reads. Another name for this strategy is "Coding the Text."

Why use Marking the Text?

Marking the Text will help students to stay engaged in their reading, to pay attention, and to remember what they've read. It helps make students' thinking visible and increases comprehension of the material.

How do I use Marking the Text?

1. Select text. Assign codes to the type of thinking in which you would like students to engage. Consult the description of the comprehension strategies presented in the previous chapter (page 40), select two or more of the Magnificent Seven Comprehension Strategies, and assign codes.

2. Model the coding process using a passage on a transparency, handout, or PowerPoint, and model your thoughts through a Think-Aloud. Show how the connections you are making help you better understand the text.

3. Assign a piece of text to the students. Have students begin to practice using the code with pieces that aren't too challenging for them. They should not only mark the text, but also describe their thinking. If they are using a textbook that they cannot mark up, students should use sticky notes or highlighting tape.

4. Start with one or two codes initially, and add more as students become more comfortable with the process.

Sample Codes

BK   *(Background knowledge):* Explanations may begin, "That reminds me of . . ."

?   *(Questions or confusing passages):* Responses may begin, "I didn't understand . . ."

I   *(Inferences or conclusions):* Responses may begin, "I think this means . . ."

P   *(Predictions):* Responses may begin, "I think what will come next . . ."

VIP   *(Very important points):* Critical ideas or phrases. Responses may begin, "A very important idea is . . ."

TS   *(Text to self connection):* Responses may begin, "This reminds of the time when I . . ."

S   *(Synthesis):* Responses may begin, "Now that I've read this, I have new ideas about . . ." or "I've changed my thinking about . . ."

TW   *(Text to world connection):* Responses may begin, "This reminds of what I saw on TV about Iraq . . ."

TT   *(Text to text connection):* Responses may begin, "This author has a different point of view than . . ."

Marginalia

What are Marginalia?

Marginalia may be the oldest strategy for interacting with text. They simply are a strategy for inserting written notes, drawings, charts, and other marks in the margins of printed text. The reader usually marks the text with symbols, words, and pictures that help him or her comprehend what he or she is reading. Creating Marginalia is a personal interaction between the reader and the text, and serves as a record of what an individual is thinking.

Why use Marginalia?

Marginalia help the reader focus during reading and remember key information. They can be used for discussion. They also personalize the text the reader is reading and allow teachers to know what the student is thinking. Marginalia that focus on the seven comprehension strategies allow students to practice reading using strategies that make a difference (Weber, 2003).

How do I use Marginalia?

1. Elaine Weber (2003) included Marginalia in Michigan Content Literacy Assessments, Standards, and Strategies (Mi CLASS), a training program for secondary teachers to promote adolescent literacy. Weber encourages teachers to demonstrate Marginalia as a Think-Aloud by using enlarged text on a transparency while demonstrating writing in the margin. First, select a short, simple piece of high-interest text of 3–6 paragraphs that will trigger use of comprehension strategies and take no more than 5 minutes to model a Think-Aloud.

2. Prepare for thinking aloud by reading the text and deciding on places within the text where you can stop and model how good readers use strategies to make sense of text.

3. Copy and enlarge the text to make a transparency for the demonstration. Leave space in the margins for writing.

4. Write your connections, questions, visualizations, inferences, and other thoughts on sticky notes.

5. Begin the mini-lesson by telling students what you are going to do; have them watch so they can analyze the process later.

6. Read and think aloud to model the comprehension strategies, and write what you're saying in the margins. You may choose to model only one comprehension strategy or more.

7. Discuss the process with students.

8. Assign a short text for students to engage in guided practice.

The following pages provide a reproducible template and examples to use with your students.

Comprehension Strategies Template

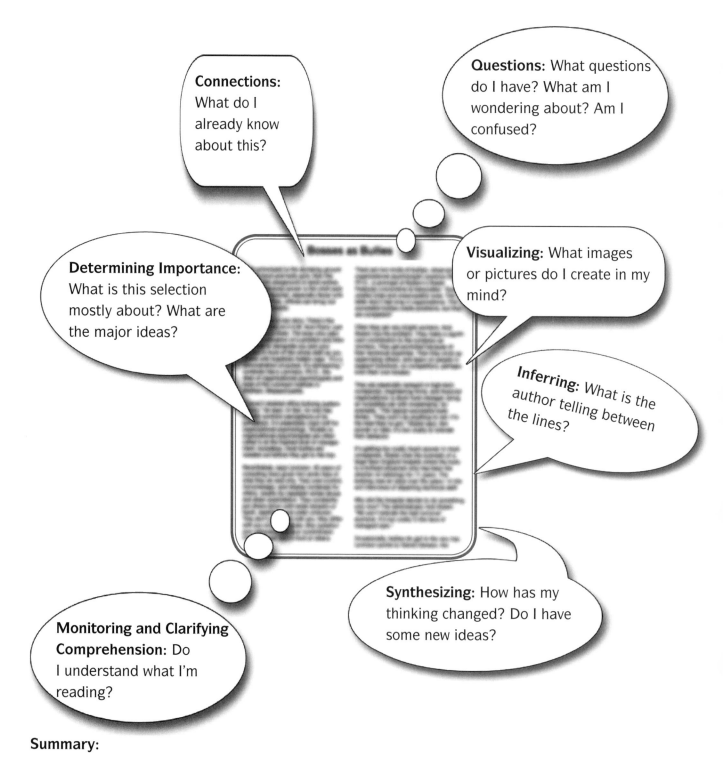

Connections: What do I already know about this?

Questions: What questions do I have? What am I wondering about? Am I confused?

Determining Importance: What is this selection mostly about? What are the major ideas?

Visualizing: What images or pictures do I create in my mind?

Inferring: What is the author telling between the lines?

Synthesizing: How has my thinking changed? Do I have some new ideas?

Monitoring and Clarifying Comprehension: Do I understand what I'm reading?

Summary:

Power Tools for Adolescent Literacy ♦ Copyright © 2009 Solution Tree Press
www.solution-tree.com ♦ Visit **go.solution-tree.com/literacy** to download this page.

Social Science Example

Connections: I already know that the Civil War was between the North and South.

Questions: Is Lincoln referring to America's Founding Fathers?

The Gettysburg Address

Four score and seven years ago our fathers brought forth on this continent, a new nation, conceived in Liberty, and dedicated to the proposition that all men are created equal.

Now we are engaged in a great civil war, testing whether that nation, or any nation so conceived and dedicated, can long endure. We are met on a great field of that war. We have come to dedicate a portion of that field, as a final resting place for those who here gave their lives that that nation might live. It is altogether fitting and proper that we should do this.

But, in a larger sense, we can not dedicate—we can not consecrate—we can not hallow—this ground. The brave men, living and dead, who struggled here, have consecrated it, far above our poor power to add or detract. The world will little note, nor long remember what we say here, but it can never forget what they did here. It is for us the living, rather, to be dedicated here to the unfinished work which they who fought here have thus far so nobly advanced. It is rather for us to be here dedicated to the great task remaining before us—that from these honored dead we take increased devotion to that cause for which they gave the last full measure of devotion—that we here highly resolve that these dead shall not have died in vain—that this nation, under God, shall have a new birth of freedom—and that government of the people, by the people, for the people, shall not perish from the earth.

Visualizing: I can just see Lincoln's sad eyes and feel his pain.

Determining Importance: The major idea here is many men died for freedom, and we can't take it for granted.

Inferring: I infer that Lincoln was a humble man who may not have thought his speech would be famous.

Monitoring and Clarifying: Do I understand what I am reading?

Synthesizing: The Revolutionary War and the Civil War were about equality and freedom.

Summary: Lincoln wanted to end the Civil War and to sustain the freedoms that our nation was founded on 87 years earlier. But he acknowledged that his words could not express the value of freedom as much as the lives of those who died at Gettysburg protecting freedom. So, President Lincoln's speech challenges all Americans to devote themselves to protecting our democracy and not take freedom for granted.

Golden Lines

What is Golden Lines?

Golden Lines is a graphic organizer designed to help students practice identifying the most important ideas, making connections, and visualizing or creating nonlinguistic representations.

Why use Golden Lines?

Golden Lines gives students a framework for determining important ideas, making connections, and visualizing during reading. It specifies the purpose for reading and sets the stage for students to pair up and have a discussion at a high level.

How do I use Golden Lines?

1. Distribute the organizer on page 85, or ask students to draw their own.

2. Ask students to read the text to identify *golden lines*—quotations or key statements that have special meaning or strike them as important.

3. Instruct students to highlight or write statements in the margins, on a sticky note, or in a journal, then make a connection to their lives, other texts, or the world.

4. Ask students to draw an illustration of the golden line in the third box.

5. Put students in pairs or groups of three and have them share each column of Golden Lines.

6. Have the students write a group summary of the key ideas.

Golden Lines Template

Golden Lines	Connections	Nonlinguistic Visual Representation

Guided Read-Aloud

What is Guided Read-Aloud?

A Guided Read-Aloud lesson provides guided practice on applying all of the Magnificent Seven Comprehension Strategies. All of the comprehension strategies are featured on a graphic organizer (page 88) and can be used with any text.

Why use Guided Read-Aloud?

The Guided Read-Aloud provides structure and focus for students who struggle with comprehension and a scaffold for practicing use of comprehension strategies. The graphic organizer (Macomb Regional Literacy Training Center, 2003) offers a way for you to "see" students' comprehension or thinking. Additionally, the graphic organizer may be used repeatedly with minor revisions with various texts.

How do I use Guided Read-Aloud?

1. Select a text that will fit with your curriculum and will interest your students. We recommend using picture books that align with topics in upper grades, are short enough for a mini-lesson, and present sophisticated ways of introducing units of study. See our list of suggested picture books categorized by content areas on pages 195–198.

2. Read the text ahead of time to practice the Read-Aloud *and* to identify the passages where you will stop and ask students to apply comprehension strategies. Use sticky notes to mark your places, and write your question or comment.

3. Customize the Guided Read-Aloud Graphic Organizer on page 88 by inserting key details of the selected text.

4. Duplicate and distribute the graphic organizer for each student.

5. Before reading, tap students' background knowledge and ask them to predict what the book will be about. Direct students to write their predictions in the first box.

6. As you read the book, stop at your pre-designated places in text, read the question or comment on the sticky note, and ask students to write their thinking or responses in the appropriate box.

7. Circulate to make sure students are on task after they record their thinking.

8. When students complete a box, you may decide how to process their responses. You may call on one or two students to share their responses, have them share with a partner or neighbor, or conduct a "whip around" the class and quickly record the responses. Alternately, you can wait until the end of the text and have the students use their graphic organizer to complete a writing assignment.

Guided Read-Aloud Graphic Organizer

Set Purposes for Reading

What does the title make you think that this is going to be about?

What do you already know about this?

Make Connections

What does this text remind you of?

Ask Questions

What questions do you have about this selection?

Make Inferences

How does _____ feel in the beginning of the story?

How does _____ feel?

Visualize

Draw one scene from the story and label it.

Determine Importance

What is the most important idea on this page?

Synthesize

What overall theme or meaning do you think would connect all the ideas in this book?

If you were to tell another person about the text in a few sentences, what would you tell them?

Use Fix-Up Strategies

When you came to a part you couldn't understand, what strategies did you use?

Power Tools for Adolescent Literacy ♦ Copyright © 2009 Solution Tree Press
www.solution-tree.com ♦ Visit **go.solution-tree.com/literacy** to download this page.

AFTER READING STRATEGIES

Strategy 3.11

Somebody Wanted But So

What is Somebody Wanted But So?

The Somebody Wanted But So (SWBS) technique helps students to identify plot elements such as conflict and resolution and provides a framework for summarizing the text (Beers, 2003). With SWBS, students complete a chart by creating a statement that identifies a character, the character's goal or motivation, a conflict that impedes the character, and the resolution of the conflict. The chart has four column headings:

Somebody (character)	Wanted (goal/motivation)	But (conflict)	So (resolution)

Why use SWBS?

While the SWBS tool is typically used after reading, it can also be used during the reading of specific chapters or a section of the text to outline the main plot as well as subplots. SWBS is a good way to summarize. It is fun and energizes students when they work together to create one or they listen to the other students share their summaries.

How do I use SWBS?

1. Model the Somebody Wanted But So technique by reading aloud a selection and showing how to fill in the four columns.

2. Next, assign a story or a chapter of a story to the class to be read silently.

3. Instruct the students to work in small groups of two or three to fill in the chart and write a statement using the information from the chart.

4. Ask each group to share the statement they have created and discuss these statements with the class.

Somebody	Wanted	But	So
Harriett Tubman	Wanted to free her people from slavery	But the journey to freedom was dangerous	So she created the Underground Railroad and led many slaves to freedom.

Read and Say Something

What is Read and Say Something?

Read and Say Something is a strategy for engaging pairs of students or small groups in reading and responding to the text. It provides a structure for partners to take turns reading and saying something about what they are reading (Short, Harste, & Burke, 1996).

Why use Read and Say Something?

Use Read and Say Something as an effective alternative to round robin reading or reading turn taking to increase active student engagement. Using this tool with partner reading will increase student engagement to a minimum of 50% because half of the class is reading at one time. Just as adults enjoy talking about what they read, adolescents benefit from conversations about text. You can roam the room to listen in and help clear up any confusion and to informally assess fluency.

How do I use Read and Say Something?

1. Use Read and Say Something after you've modeled the comprehension strategies and when students have experienced using the thinking strategies. Students should be comfortable using the language of the comprehension strategies included on the Reciprocal Teaching Role Cards (see page 59).

2. Select a text and read it to decide how to chunk the text—by paragraph or page.

3. Assign or allow students to choose partners and distribute materials, including the text and sets of the Reciprocal Teaching Role Cards, if available.

4. Ask students to decide who will be A and who B; explain that half of the class will read aloud at the same time and to read and say something quietly.

5. Reader A goes first and reads aloud the first paragraph or chunk of text. The other student reads along also and "says something" after the first paragraph: clarifies, questions, predicts, or summarizes. Reader A may

respond and the partners may have a conversation, or they may go on to the next paragraph and Reader B reads aloud.

6. This process continues throughout the text as partners take turns reading and saying something. Roam the room to monitor and support students in discussing the text.

7. End the experience by asking students to collaborate on a summary of the important ideas from the text.

Even Dozen

What is Even Dozen?

Even Dozen is a tool for summarizing and synthesizing material that has been read. It's an effective process for reviewing content in small groups. Even Dozen can be used to synthesize information from articles, presentations, books, and so on.

Why use Even Dozen?

Even Dozen reveals what students think are key concepts or ideas and helps students to see relationships among the ideas.

How do I use Even Dozen?

1. After giving students time to read a selection of text, divide them into groups of five students. Ask each group to draw a large square with 12 boxes on large chart paper.

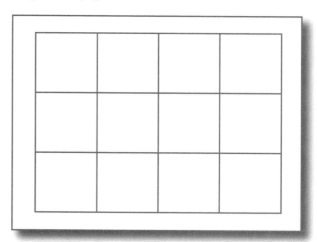

2. Next, ask each group to reflect on the content of the text, to identify 12 critical ideas, concepts, or principles from the text, and to write one idea in each block.

3. Once all the boxes have been completed, the first student in the group chooses one of the boxes. The student then reviews with the others in the group what they know about the key idea in the box and writes "#1" in the box.

4. Going clockwise, the second student selects a box, explains what the group knows, and writes "#2" in the square. Then, the second student must tell how the idea in box #2 connects or relates to the idea in box #1.

5. The third student selects a box, explains what they know, and then has to connect that box to box #1 and box #2.

6. The group keeps going until the last box is explained and connected. The group synthesizes the ideas by reporting each concept and then linking each idea.

7. Allow students to help each other at any time in this review. They should also be allowed to use their notes or textbook, or to ask you for information or clarification.

Save the Last Word for Me

What is Save the Last Word for Me?

Save the Last Word for Me (SLWM) is a structure for discussion that emphasizes reading, reviewing, and making sense of text (Harste, Shorte, & Burke, 1996). The process requires students to find a sentence, paragraph, or segment of the text that "strikes" them or that they find especially interesting. Alternatively, the teacher can specify something for students to look for and select. SLWM also requires students to discuss their choices of selected text, explain, and defend them.

Why use Save the Last Word for Me?

SLWM gives students a focus and purpose for reading and encourages students to participate in discussions to share ideas and opinions about the text. SLWM asks readers to connect to a passage in an emotional way, and emotions impact memory.

How do I use Save the Last Word for Me?

1. Ask students to read an article, newspaper passage, chapter, or text passage. As students read the text, they each identify a statement or quote that they would like to discuss. The selected statements could be statements with which they agree or disagree, or ones they find puzzling, surprising, or highly interesting.

2. Have the students copy their selected statements and record the page number of the segment onto a 3 x 5 note card.

3. Then ask students to write a paragraph on the back of the card for each statement or quote, explaining why they selected the statements.

4. Divide the class into small groups. Each group selects a student to begin the process, and that student reads one of his or her selected statements to the group.

5. Then the student turns his or her card over and reads what he or she has written about and why this particular selection was made—what the student thinks or feels about the statement.

6. Each member of the group responds to the statement by describing what they think the statement means. Tell the other students that

if they disagree with the choice, they must express their reasons for disagreeing.

7. Tell the class that the "last word" is "saved" for the student who made the selection, and he or she may choose to either alter or stand by the choice.

8. The discussion of the text continues with each member of the group taking a turn sharing their statements and thinking.

9. After all students have discussed their cards, the groups report out to the whole class by selecting one card to present.

10. You may ask students to use the following checklist to assess their work.

Checklist for Participation in SLWM	Yes or No	Comment
Reads and makes sense of the text		
Completes assigned reading and SLWM to the best of ability		
Participates in SLWM discussion		
Provides at least two reasons for choosing his or her passage		
Contributes thoughtful comments to SLWM group discussion		
Listens attentively and responds appropriately to peer comments in discussion		

Foldables

What are Foldables?

Foldables are journals and writing materials that students construct to create hands-on structures for organizing information. Examples of different ways to fold paper include hamburger, hotdog, layered, accordion, tri-fold, and shutterfold. Foldables are one way of helping students integrate reading, writing, thinking, organizing data, researching, and other communication skills into various content areas.

Why use Foldables?

Foldables organize information in a way that makes it easier for students to grasp major concepts and remember information. They replace teacher-generated writing or photocopied sheets with student-constructed booklets and student-generated print, forcing the student to interact with the content and creating a sense of student ownership. They can also be used as an assessment of student learning. Student-made Foldables using construction paper engage adolescents in a fun, hands-on activity and are a cost-efficient way to create study guides for note-taking.

How do I use Foldables?

1. Select essential content to be taught, and identify and list the topic and major headings or categories for each section of the Foldable.

2. Select the best type of Foldable for the content that will be learned: a layered look book or a four-panel Foldable. See a variety of options created by Dinah Zike for middle school math, science, and history at www.dinah.com.

3. Distribute the materials (8.5 x 11 paper).

4. Practice folding and giving directions, as this is not as easy as it looks! Allow extra time the first time you use Foldables in class, too.

5. Teach students to write general information—titles, ideas, questions—on the tabs of their Foldables.

Layered Look Book Directions

1

Stack two sheets of paper, and shift the bottom sheet to stick out 1" higher than the top sheet. (If you stack more than two sheets, use less than 1" between sheets.)

2

Gently fold the sheets, and align the edges so that all the layers (the "tabs") are the same distance apart.

3

When all tabs are an equal distance apart, crease well.

4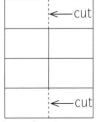

To finish the Foldable, either staple along the outside edges or glue the sheets together at the center fold.

Four-Panel Foldable Directions

1

fold

Fold a sheet of paper in half lengthwise.

2

fold

Fold the sheet in half again to make a rectangle.

3

fold

Fold the sheet in half a third time.

4

← cut

← cut

Unfold the sheet and cut as shown on the dotted lines.

5

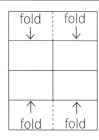

Fold the top and bottom flaps toward the middle.

6

Term	Term
Term	Term

Direct students to write a term on each of the four outside flaps.

7 Finally, have students lift up each flap to work on the inside of the Foldable. Ask them to write a definition and create an illustration for each term on the inside.

Readers' Theater

What is Readers' Theater?

Readers' Theater is a way to make content curriculum and books come alive for all types of readers and serves as a viable alternative to round-robin reading. Readers' Theater can involve individuals, pairs, or small groups in chorally reading identified parts or roles. Excerpts from textbooks, informational text, picture books, or other resources may be rewritten into a script. The teacher assigns parts or roles that students read orally.

Why use Readers' Theater?

Students love to perform, and Readers' Theater is a fun and risk-free way to get them to enjoy reading and rereading the content. Readers' Theater is an effective strategy for improving fluent reading, comprehension, and writing, and the repetition increases retention of content (Rasinski, 2003).

How do I use Readers' Theater?

1. Search the Internet for sources of ready-made scripts, or create your own using a variety of types of texts. Look for stories that are simple and lively, with lots of dialogue or action, and not too many scenes or characters. Any story can be transformed into a theatrical performance, but some are easier to work with than others. Scripts can also be created from content-area texts as illustrated by the example at the end of this description. Find picture books connected to content objectives, and ask students to create scripts. Readers' Theater is more effective when students prepare their own scripts because they must review the curriculum material and determine the most important information and ideas. This writing activity also integrates reading, writing, and thinking skills.

2. Make copies of the script for students.

3. Model and provide instructions for students for how to read the scripts. Students should always read silently first and then practice reading aloud their parts before performing. Highlighting their parts will help.

4. Provide students with performance tips such as "Face the audience" and "Speak clearly and with expression while reading."

Doing the Wave: A Sample Script

Following is a sample script taken from Rosalind Flynn's book *Dramatizing the Content With Curriculum-Based Readers Theatre* (2007) that makes learning about the science of light and sound waves a theatrical experience. Used with permission of the International Reading Association.

All: *We're here to tell you about The Wave!*

All: *[Gesturing and making the noise of the stadium "wave"]*

First speaker: *Not that kind of wave!*

All: *[Making noises of confusion]*

First speaker: *Wave as in light and sound waves!*

All: *Ohhhhh. [Gesturing]*

Second speaker: *There are many different parts to a wave.*

Third speaker: *What kinds of parts?*

Fourth speaker: *Duh, haven't you heard?*

Second speaker: *There's amplitude!*

Third speaker: *Ampli–what?*

All: *Amplitude! [Sound effect]*

Fifth speaker: *And you better improve your attitude, son!*

Third speaker: *Yes, sir!*

Fifth speaker: *Amplitude is the height of a wave from its midpoint.*

All: *Amplitude [Sound effect]—the height of a wave from its midpoint.*

Third speaker: *Can you put that in my terms?*

Sixth speaker: *[Whispers] I hate learning about these boring waves.*

Seventh speaker: *Shhhhh!*

Fifth speaker: *Amplitude indicates the amount of energy carried in the wave.*

Power Tools for Adolescent Literacy ♦ Copyright © 2009 Solution Tree Press
www.solution-tree.com ♦ Visit **go.solution-tree.com/literacy** to download this page.

Readers' Theater Presentation Rubric

(Created for Project CLASS by Cindy Bridges [2006c] and used with permission.)

Name: _____ Date: _____

	Excellent (8–10 points)	Good (4–7 points)	Needs Work (0–3 points)
Reads With Volume	Consistently speaks loudly enough for audience to hear	Usually speaks loudly enough for audience to hear	Speaks too soft or loud to hear
Reads With Clarity	Pronounces words correctly and is easily understood	Pronounces most words correctly and is easily understood	Pronounces many words incorrectly, talks too fast or slow, mumbles
Reads With Expression	Consistently reads with appropriate expression	Usually reads with appropriate expression	Reads with little or no expression
Reads in Turn	Takes turns accurately on a consistent basis	Takes turns accurately on a somewhat consistent basis	Takes turns rarely on a consistent basis
Cooperates With Group	Consistently works well with others	Sometimes works well with others	Difficulty in working with others

Comments:

_____

_____

_____

_____

_____

Total points possible: 40   Points earned: _____   Percentage: _____ %

Reflection and Application

Review the strategies in this chapter for increasing reading comprehension, and select three to five strategies that you plan to try. Begin by thinking about your existing lessons. Which strategy can you add to an existing lesson plan? You may also want to think about identifying specific standards or objectives with which you will use the strategies. Alternatively, what tool can you change or modify for your classroom?

Teacher Tools	What do I NOT want to try?	How can I add this to an existing lesson?	What different standards can I use it with?	What tool can I change or use another way?
Scavenger Hunt				
Passage Prediction				
Anticipation Guide				
Reading Aloud Picture Books				
Interactive Notebooks				
Mind Mapping				
Marking the Text				
Marginalia				
Golden Lines				
Guided Read-Aloud				
Somebody Wanted But So				
Read and Say Something				

Teacher Tools	What do I NOT want to try?	How can I add this to an existing lesson?	What different standards can I use it with?	What tool can I change or use another way?
Even Dozen				
Save the Last Word for Me				
Foldables				
Readers' Theater				

Notes for lesson planning:

Chapter 4

Developing Vocabulary

> *Teaching vocabulary well is a key aspect of developing engaged and successful readers.*
>
> —*Karen D'Angelo Bromley*

A major challenge for Mr. Love in supporting all students' success in learning ninth-grade science is the technical vocabulary essential for comprehending the science textbook. He accepts the fact that assigning the entire list of vocabulary words from the chapter is not effective, and selects and teaches a few words using direct instruction.

Before presenting new and challenging vocabulary from the science textbook, Mr. Love assessed his students' prior knowledge of five key words related to the functioning of the kidney by asking students to rate their level of knowledge from "clueless" to "could teach it." Finding that most students were unfamiliar with the words, he described the terms in user-friendly words, gave examples, and asked students to write descriptions of the terms in their own words in their academic vocabulary notebooks. Then he acted out the words using a nonlinguistic approach and graphics to illustrate the terms' meanings. Next, students created their own pictures representing the new terms. A couple of the words were difficult for students to pronounce, but they were highly engaged with their vocabulary partners as they shared their definitions and pictures.

To conclude the lesson, Mr. Love asked small groups to write and act out a summary statement on how kidneys function using the newly learned words. After school, Mr. Love reviewed the student responses on Exit Tickets to assess their level of understanding on the new concepts and to plan his instruction for the next day. He will engage small groups in a word-sort activity to deepen word knowledge while he conferences with students who are struggling.

Vocabulary development is a critical issue. As students progress across the grades, the vocabulary gap widens between the children of economically disadvantaged homes and the children from advantaged homes, where they hear more than twice the number of words spoken as their peers. We also know that students require multiple exposures to learn and retain new words, with struggling readers needing *more* than the average 14 exposures.

Teachers are searching for vocabulary instructional strategies that work to replace the traditional strategies that don't work. We've all experienced the ineffectiveness of assigning a long list of words for students to look up, copy the definitions from the dictionary or glossary, and then use the words in sentences. Another common practice with ineffective results is using worksheets or workbooks for vocabulary; students use those words out of context, commit them only to short-term memory, and quickly forget them.

Vocabulary development is not the exclusive job of the language arts teacher. Vocabulary instruction raises reading comprehension; thus, *all* content teachers need to teach specialized words that are critical to their discipline.

Suggested Resources

Allen, J. (1999). *Words, words, words.* Portland, ME: Stenhouse.

Beck, I., McKeown, M., & Kucan, L. (2002). *Bringing words to life.* New York: Guilford.

Blachowicz, C., & Fisher, P. (2002). *Teaching vocabulary in all classrooms* (2nd ed.). Upper Saddle River, NJ: Prentice Hall.

Bromley, K. (2002). *Stretching students' vocabulary, grades 3–8.* New York: Scholastic.

Graves, M. (2005). *The vocabulary book.* Urbana, IL: Teachers College.

Marzano, R., & Pickering, D. (2004). *Building academic vocabulary.* Alexandria, VA: Association for Supervision and Curriculum Development.

Marzano, R., & Pickering, D. (2005). *Building academic vocabulary: Teacher's manual.* Alexandria, VA: Association for Supervision and Curriculum Development.

Nagy, W. E. (1988). *Teaching vocabulary to improve reading comprehension.* Urbana, IL: National Council of Teachers of English, and Newark, DE: International Reading Association.

Pilgreen, J. L. (2000). *The SSR handbook.* Portsmouth, NH: Boynton/Cook Publishers.

Rasinski, T., et al. (2000). *Teaching word recognition, spelling, and vocabulary.* Newark, DE: International Reading Association.

Did You Know?

♦ Students learn a lot of words when teachers immerse them in words.

♦ Students remember words when they are actively engaged with them.

♦ Sustained, silent reading is a powerful way to build background knowledge and vocabulary.

♦ Students learn an average of 3,000 to 4,000 words per school year (Nagy, Anderson, & Herman, 1987).

♦ Students learn words when they describe them in their own words instead of copying the definition given by the text or the teacher.

♦ Students learn words when they create nonlinguistic representations of the words.

♦ Students learn words when they are given periodic opportunities to use the words and talk about terms with each other, and when they play games with the words.

♦ All words cannot be taught either through direct or incidental instruction. The gap in students' vocabularies when they enter school is extensive (Hart & Risley, 1995), and students encounter 180,000 words in school texts (Zeno et al., 1995).

♦ Strategic selection of vocabulary is essential to close the gap. Vocabulary instruction should focus on content-specific terms that support academic success (Marzano, 2004).

Direct Vocabulary Instruction

What is Direct Vocabulary Instruction?

Direct Vocabulary Instruction is an intentional process for teaching strategically selected terms. Direct instruction is explicit, intentional teaching. Teachers model how to unlock the meaning of unfamiliar words through brief, 5–10 minute Think-Alouds that make the process transparent by showing, not telling. Marzano's (2004) six-step process for direct instruction presents a framework for how English, math, science, and social science teachers can use the same approach to increase student success.

Why use Direct Vocabulary Instruction?

When implemented collaboratively by all content teachers within a school, Marzano's (2004) six-step process enhances the probability of students' academic success. Vocabulary knowledge strongly influences comprehension (Beck, McKeown, & Omanson, 1987) and while content teachers cannot directly teach all the words that students need for success, they can show students strategies for unlocking words independently. Success on state achievement tests requires high-level vocabulary. Reading and understanding college textbooks demands a more extensive vocabulary.

How do I use Direct Vocabulary Instruction?

The following is a description of Marzano's six steps for instruction.

1. Describe the word, and provide an explanation and an example for each new term. Avoid the traditional but ineffective approach of relying on definitions or activities such as looking up words in the dictionary, writing the definition, and using the new word in a sentence. Use everyday language to describe the new word, and provide key features so you don't sound like a dictionary. Effective instruction is about helping students figure out how words are like other words and how they are different from other words.

2. Ask students to write a description of the new term's meaning in their own words rather than copying your explanation. Some schools ask students to maintain an academic notebook for each content area that contains graphic organizers with three columns: *My Description, Graphic*

Representation, and *New Insight.* This step corresponds to the first column: *My Description* is the student's explanation.

3. Next, students construct a visual or nonlinguistic representation of the term such as a graphic organizer, picture, pictograph, or map. Students need to hear, see, read, and use terms orally to develop meaning and use.

4. Engage students in a variety of activities that provide multiple exposures with the terms: comparing, contrasting, making metaphors and analogies, revising initial descriptions or nonlinguistic representations, and creating roots and affixes. Engage in vertical planning with teachers in your school to determine which roots and affixes will be systematically taught in which grades. Use graphic organizers such as vocabulary trees to help students learn roots.

5. Provide time for students to discuss the new words and share their visuals, challenging words, favorite words, questions, and other information from their vocabulary notebooks with partners or small groups.

6. Use games as practice and review activities and tools for vocabulary development. Take advantage of students' sense of play and discovery by using word puzzles. Provide opportunities for multiple exposures, and stimulate interest and enthusiasm for words by being a positive model and lover of words.

Read-Alouds

What are Read-Alouds?

A Read-Aloud is a planned oral reading of a book, article, or excerpt from a text and is usually related to a theme or topic of study. We encourage content teachers to establish reading aloud as a classroom routine as a way to introduce good books, magazines, and newspapers and provide students with a model of fluency. An excellent source for information on Read-Alouds is located at Jim Trelease's website: www.trelease-on-reading.com.

Why use Read-Alouds?

Language development starts with students listening and developing oral vocabulary and evolves to reading and writing vocabulary. Read-Aloud expert Jim Trelease (2001) asserts that Read-Alouds prepare students for success on the SAT because students will read and write words learned through rich literature. The Read-Aloud can be used to develop background knowledge, introduce new concepts, and increase vocabulary. A Read-Aloud can be used to model the use of strategies that promote comprehension. Students who struggle to read need good fluency models and gain from listening to text that would not be accessible to them.

How do I use Read-Alouds?

1. Select a book based on a specific purpose; this purpose could be developing concept background, introducing key vocabulary, or just sharing highly engaging text.

2. Choose an article, poem, or section of a book that lends itself to being read aloud, supports your objective, and contains desired concepts and vocabulary. Read the selection and identify words, phrases, and sentences that you will emphasize and stop and talk about during the Read-Aloud. You may want to mark these spots with sticky notes and write notes or questions. It is important to read the text *before* you read it to your class.

3. Picture books are excellent sources for introducing units of study. As you read, move around the room so that students can see the illustrations, or use a document camera to project the text and illustrations as you read aloud.

4. Read with expression to show students what fluent readers sound like.

5. Introduce the title of the text and/or cover, and ask students to turn to a partner and predict what the text is about.

6. Tell students why you are reading aloud and state the purpose for listening:

   Listen to the picture book Teammates *[Golenbock, 1990], to identify words that help us to define the concept of segregation.*

   (A sample lesson plan that uses a Read-Aloud of the picture book *Teammates* and emphasizes vocabulary and concept development is included in the appendix [pages 183–184]).

7. Stop during the Read-Aloud at predesignated segments to think aloud and talk about word meanings, but do not overdo the stopping points.

8. Discuss the text and ask what students learned; connect their prior knowledge to the new.

Implement a 1-minute Read-Aloud as a routine that begins or ends instruction daily, using books like *The Worst-Case Scenario Book of Survival Questions* (Piven & Borgenicht, 2005) as high-interest text for short Read-Alouds (Gallagher, 2008). Model the 1-minute Read-Aloud for a couple of months, and then turn the Read-Aloud routine over to students. Gallagher recommends having a stash of materials for students to select text in the event students forget or are absent.

A list of picture books recommended for content areas is located on pages 195–198.

Sustained Silent Reading

What is Sustained Silent Reading?

Sustained Silent Reading (SSR) is uninterrupted 20- to 30-minute sessions allotted daily, ideally, for independent reading of books or other materials that match student interest and reading ability.

Why use Sustained Silent Reading?

Wide reading contributes approximately 25–50% of vocabulary development per year (Nagy, Anderson, & Herman, 1987). SSR programs that are implemented continuously, consistently, and systematically over many years increase reading comprehension and motivation (Pilgreen, 2000).

How do I use Sustained Silent Reading?

The first step in implementing an effective schoolwide SSR program is teacher agreement across grades and content areas (Marzano, 2004). A comprehensive resource for schools on steps for implementing SSR is Pilgreen's *The SSR Handbook: How to Organize and Manage a Sustained Silent Reading Program* (2000). SSR programs make a difference when:

- ◆ Schedules provide uninterrupted time to read of about 20- to 30-minute sessions at least twice a week or more.

- ◆ Programs promote student choice of material and topics.

- ◆ Students write and talk to others about their reading.

Anticipating Words

(From The Learning Communities Guide to Improving Reading Instruction *by Valerie Gregory and Jan Rozzelle [Corwin, 2005] and used with permission.)*

What is Anticipating Words?

Anticipating Words is a strategy to engage students in creating a list of words that they expect to encounter in the text, based on its title or images provided by the teacher.

Why use Anticipating Words?

Anticipating Words helps students make connections among words and reinforces reading with purpose. It gives students a strategy for activating background knowledge prior to reading (Allen, 2002).

How do I use Anticipating Words?

1. Identify words in expository text that may represent barriers to students' comprehension, and write the beginning letter of each word in a list.

2. Give students the title of the text (or an illustration, such as a photograph of the rain forest) and your list of the beginning letters of selected words. Tell students that the letters represent words that are important to understanding the text, and are clues for predicting words they will find in the article.

3. In small groups, students brainstorm words they predict they will see and record their words in journals, on individual 3 x 5 cards for each letter, or on charts.

4. Students share their words before reading the text, return to their lists after reading the text to compare their words with actual words they encountered in the text, and then discuss words from their lists that could be substituted in the text.

Teaching Word Parts

What is Teaching Word Parts?

Teaching Word Parts is providing direct instruction on the most frequent prefixes, suffixes, and roots. It is a part of effective vocabulary instruction that provides students with strategies for figuring out unfamiliar words independently. Teaching Word Parts is the structural analysis of words to determine the meaning of individual morphemes or smallest parts.

Why use Teaching Word Parts?

There are a few affixes that have constant meanings and consistent spellings that are used in a majority of words. As Marzano notes, "Knowledge of roots and affixes enables students to determine the meaning of unknown words" (2004, p. 76). If teachers focused on teaching the four most frequent prefixes (*un-, re-, in-,* and *dis-*), they would help students figure out 58% of prefixed words; similarly, just four suffixes (*-is, -es, -ed,* and *-ing*) account for 65% of suffixed words (Marzano, 2004) .

How do I use Teaching Word Parts?

White, Sowell, and Yanagilhara (in Marzano, 2004, p. 77) emphasize teaching the most common prefixes in a series of mini-lessons.

1. In the first lesson, introduce the concept of prefix, explain it, and provide examples and nonexamples of prefixes.

2. Present the prefixes *un-* and *dis-* in the second lesson, and explain their negative meanings: "not" or "the opposite of." Provide several examples, such as *disagree, disconnect, disappear, unequal,* and *unable.* Use the example words in sentences:

    Students disagree on the best movie.

    Then define the whole word:

    To disagree means to not agree, to think differently, to hold different opinions.

    Follow this procedure for the other prefixes, as described in the next steps.

3. In the third lesson, introduce the negative meanings of *in-, im-, ir-,* and *non-.* Provide several examples of each, such as *incomplete, impartial, irresponsible,* and *nonsense.*

4. Next, present the prefix *re-* with definitions ("back" and "again") and examples (*return* and *reconsider*) in the fourth lesson.

5. The fifth lesson emphasizes the less common meanings of *un-* and *dis-* ("do the opposite") and *in-* and *im-* ("in" or "into").

6. The sixth lesson focuses on the meanings of and examples for *en-, em-,* and *mis-* (*enroll, embed, misunderstand*).

7. Have students break down words into chunks, define each part, and then create a description of the meaning, as in the following example for the word *imported.*

im	port	ed
into	to carry	in the past

Guide the discussion toward the realization that *imported* probably means that something was carried into someplace.

The Frayer Model

What is the Frayer Model?

The Frayer Model (Frayer, Frederick, & Klausmeier, 1969) is a graphic organizer that helps students to understand the meaning of a new concept and to distinguish what the concept is and what it is not. The four quadrants of the graphic may contain slightly different headings, but in general they require learners to first analyze and list essential and nonessential characteristics (or "traits" and "definition"), and later to consider and list examples and nonexamples from their own lives to further clarify their understanding of the word.

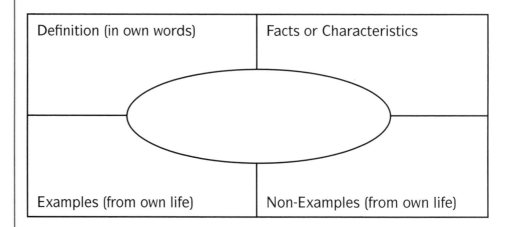

Why use the Frayer Model?

The Frayer Model is a comprehensive procedure for teaching new words and is especially useful in introducing concepts before and after reading a text. This approach helps students to compare and contrast concepts, and to understand how words are like and different from other words. It is particularly beneficial in teaching difficult concepts. The Frayer Model was designed to assess the level of concept mastery.

How do I use the Frayer Model?

1. Introduce the concept being studied, and give students a graphic organizer similar to those at the end of this section.

2. Explain the structure and all the attributes of the Frayer Model.

3. Complete a simple model with the whole class.

For example, use the concept of "fairness," and ask students for words that characterize "fairness." List responses on a whiteboard, overhead, or chart paper so that all students can see the responses. Ask students for examples of fairness from their lives (responses may include things like "sharing a pizza evenly"), and write a few as enlarged text. Next, ask students to consider what fairness is *not,* and to turn to their partner and share an example of something that happened to them that was unfair. (An example might be a time when a parent punished one sibling for something that another sibling had done.) Last, discuss and write a definition in the appropriate block of the graphic organizer.

4. Have students work in pairs to complete a model in guided practice.

5. Have students share their work.

Sample Frayer Model for Science

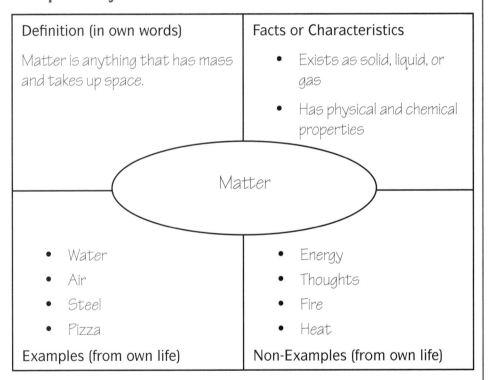

Definition (in own words)	Facts or Characteristics
Matter is anything that has mass and takes up space.	• Exists as solid, liquid, or gas • Has physical and chemical properties

Matter

Examples (from own life)	Non-Examples (from own life)
• Water • Air • Steel • Pizza	• Energy • Thoughts • Fire • Heat

Sample Frayer Model for Mathematics: Polygon

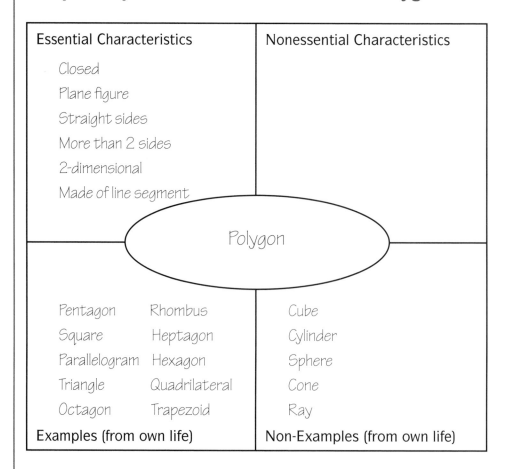

Essential Characteristics	Nonessential Characteristics
Closed	
Plane figure	
Straight sides	
More than 2 sides	
2-dimensional	
Made of line segment	

Polygon

Pentagon	Rhombus	Cube
Square	Heptagon	Cylinder
Parallelogram	Hexagon	Sphere
Triangle	Quadrilateral	Cone
Octagon	Trapezoid	Ray
Examples (from own life)		Non-Examples (from own life)

Strategy 4.7

Concept Maps

What are Concept Maps?

Concept Maps are graphic organizers that show the relationships among several concepts and promote understanding of a word's many levels of meaning. They go beyond dictionary definitions and encourage the application of personal knowledge (Ryder & Graves, 2003).

Why use Concept Maps?

Concept Maps help to preteach difficult concepts and vocabulary at all grade levels, and intermediate and middle school students can use them on their own to deepen knowledge. Concept Maps provide opportunities for students to interact with related terms, see relationships, and organize their thinking for writing. Concept Maps are useful to assess prior knowledge of concepts; completed maps are also useful as study guides and organizers for writing.

How do I use Concept Maps?

1. Start by displaying a blank map on the overhead or board; in the center, write a familiar concept or word. Ask for a definition of the word. (Do several easy examples to teach the process, and guide students in completing their own maps of easy words.)

2. Decide on the structure that fits your content best, and design your organizer. Complete the organizer by pulling information from the textbook and other sources *before* introducing the concept to your class. Completing the map will help you organize the delivery of the content.

3. Give students a copy of the graphic organizer. Tell students that they are responsible for writing and organizing information on the Concept Map, but you will guide them.

4. Model how to complete the Concept Map on the overhead or whiteboard.

    To describe how to use Concept Maps, we'll use the "Branches of Government" example that Cindy Bridges used in her eighth-grade history classroom (see the reproducible on page 121). Ask students to write in the names of the three branches on the graphic organizer. Provide one key responsibility for each branch of the government, and check for understanding.

5. Organize students in pairs or groups, and direct them to read the text to determine additional characteristics and responsibilities of each branch and to record the information in the appropriate branch.

6. When students understand how to use the Concept Map, give them a new concept from the curriculum, and have them work in pairs to create their own maps. Encourage students to use information from the glossary, dictionary, and their own background knowledge. Then, using all their information, ask students to write a summary or description of the concept that is fuller and more meaningful than the one in the dictionary.

Concept Map

(Created for Project CLASS by Cindy Bridges [2006a] and used with permission.)

Name _____ Date _____

What is it?

(category)

(property)

(property)

Branches of Government
(concept)

(property)

(property)

What are some examples?

(illustration)

(illustration)

(illustration)

New Definition: _____

_____

_____

Concept Sorts

What are Concept Sorts?

In a Concept Sort, students sort words into different categories to learn or review words. Teachers may use a *closed* sort or *open* sort. In a closed sort, the teacher provides the categories into which students sort the words. In an open sort, students create their own labels for categories after sorting the words. The open sort is more difficult.

Why use Concept Sorts?

Content terms may be learned when students manipulate words in paired and group activities requiring categorization (Beck, McKeown, & Kucan, 2002). Concept Sorts help students understand relationships and make connections among key words and concepts (Gillett & Temple, 1983). They are helpful:

- ♦ As advance organizers before reading

- ♦ As a reflection and review activity after reading

- ♦ To organize ideas before writing

- ♦ To preteach vocabulary and technical terms in all subject areas

- ♦ To assess and provide background knowledge before embarking on a new unit of study

How do I use Concept Sorts?

1. Identify your content area topic, and compile a list of 12 to 30 related words, depending on your students' level, and write the words on index cards. Students copy terms onto index cards or cut premade words from your teacher-made lists. Alternatively, type the words on a template like those that follow in this chapter and reproduce the handout for groups to cut and categorize.

2. For difficult concepts, use a closed sort; introduce the categories, and ask students to sort the words. If words and concepts are easier, or if the activity is a review, use an open sort; ask students to find the labels or categories and then sort the words to fit the categories.

3. Students may work in pairs, groups, or independently. When working with a partner or group, students say the words repeatedly, which helps them learn the words.

4. Students may glue the words into their academic vocabulary notebook for small word sorts or on a piece of construction paper or poster for the Community Learning Wall.

Sample Math Open Concept Sort

triangle	line	square	ray
radius	obtuse angle	perimeter	rectangle
diameter	rhombus	circumference	isosceles triangle
angle	right angle	parallelogram	degrees
area			

Sample Language Arts Concept Sort

questioned	called	melancholy	gloomy
traveled	forlorn	woeful	replied
stated	asked	shouted	whispered
lumbered	diminutive	small	mournful
crestfallen	sorrowful	miserable	hilarious
ambled	mammoth	dejected	laughable
witty	immense	enormous	huge
towering	minuscule	exclaimed	remarked
depressed	marched	cried	responded
demanded	sidesplitting	humorous	microscopic
colossal	amusing	giant	gigantic
staggered	strutted	tiny	compact
downcast	hiked	paraded	

Sample Social Studies
Closed Concept Sort: Movements

(Bridges, 2006f)

Suffrage Movement	Reduced work hours	Freedom Riders	End slavery
18th Amendment	Increased educational opportunities	Boycotts and sit-ins	Harriet Tubman
Rosa Parks	Workplace reform	Alcohol	Abolitionist Movement
Improved safety conditions	William Lloyd Garrison	Speakeasies	Montgomery Bus Boycott
Elizabeth Cady Stanton	Passive resistance	Voting rights for women	Progressive Movement
Voting Rights Act of 1965	Temperance Movement	Brown v. Board of Education	*The Liberator*
Placed restrictions on child labor	19th Amendment	Prohibition	Bootlegging
Civil Rights Movement	NAACP	Martin Luther King, Jr.	Susan B. Anthony
Frederick Douglass			

Sample Science Concept Sort:
Physical Properties

(Dunn, 2006a)

shape	vaporization	adjustment knob	gas
color	boiling	100's slider	smell
evaporation	freezing	ductibility	taste
texture	10's slider	melting	buoyancy
1's slider	pointer	condensation	sublimation
deposition	"testable" physical properties	conductivity	phase or state changes
solid	qualitative observations	liquid	solubility
parts of a triple beam balance	pan	phases or states of matter	

Math Concept Sort

(Created for Project CLASS by Amy Lamb [2006a] and used with permission.)

Cut out the column headings below, and glue them onto your construction paper. Leave some space between each column heading. Then write each number from the number list under its correct column heading. Keep in mind that you may need to put a number in more than one category. Finally, work with a partner to make up two additional numbers for each column, and write those last.

Column Headings

a whole number that is not a natural number	rational numbers that are not whole, natural, or integers
integers that are not whole numbers	irrational numbers

rational numbers	natural numbers	real numbers

Number List

18	31	5/8
-7.32	2.3333 . . .	Square root of 16
½	9.8	4.563218954 . . .
6.8	Square root of 12	0
1.5	-99	-45
-78	15/3	12
72.6	35%	

List, Group, Label

What is List, Group, Label?

Originally used for science and social studies vocabulary (Taba, 1967), the List, Group, Label activity directs students to list all the vocabulary they know around a given topic, then organize those words, and finally to create a label that summarizes the group's shared characteristics.

Why use List, Group, Label?

This activity uses categorization to teach students to organize their verbal concepts. List, Group, Label may be used with the whole class, small groups, or individually.

How do I use List, Group, Label?

1. Introduce the new concept or unit of study, and ask students to think of all the words they know that are related to the topic. You may decide to allow students to use their text, if they need help to brainstorm words.

2. Next, ask students to organize the words into groups.

3. Finally, ask students to give each group a label: for example, *measurement tools, space figures, words with six letters, words beginning with "s," curved surfaces,* and so on.

4. You may choose to exhibit the words on a word wall and ask students to add to the clusters of words as they continue to learn about the topic.

Strategy 4.10

Linear Array

What is a Linear Array?

Linear Arrays are visual representations of degree or gradations (Allen, 1999). Shandra Dunn, science teacher at Berkeley Middle School in Williamsburg, Virginia, calls them "serial words" in her science classroom and gives her students a list of words that they must place in some kind of order that they can explain. For example, students could place math words for shapes in a series according to the number of sides each shape has.

Why use a Linear Array?

Linear Arrays help the student to see how words are related in a tangible, tactile, hands-on, engaging fashion. Manipulating a series of words gives students experience in thinking about and using the terms as they create a logical order for arranging the words. This experience provides students with deeper insights for the terms.

How do I use a Linear Array?

Give students a series of words on cards, and ask them to arrange the words in some kind of order. For example, words could be organized in order of difficulty for the student from "clueless" to "could teach it."

Sample Science Linear Array

Arrange these words in order of phase of matter.

liquid   solid   gas   plasma

| plasma | ( ) | | ( ) |

Sample Math Linear Array

Arrange these polygon words according to the number of sides in the shape.

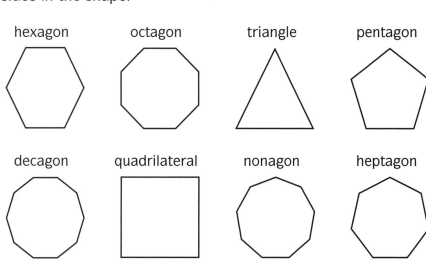

| hexagon | octagon | triangle | pentagon |

| decagon | quadrilateral | nonagon | heptagon |

Mystery Word of the Day

What is Mystery Word of the Day?

Mystery Word of the Day is a fast-paced game designed to introduce new words. It requires students to brainstorm words that fit several clues designed and presented by the teacher. As students play with vocabulary words, they must eliminate words that do not make sense.

Why use Mystery Word of the Day?

It is fun! It's a good "bell ringer" or opening and a quick way to learn how words are used in different contexts and assume multiple meanings. This activity can engender a love for learning and manipulating words.

How do I use Mystery Word of the Day?

1. Select a word or concept that is correlated to your content and that may be challenging for students to learn because of its complexity.

2. Create five or six clues or sentences with blanks where the word would fit. Create a PowerPoint slide or transparency for each clue, and add graphics.

3. Present the first clue. This should be a clue likely to generate many words—a sentence where many words could fill in the blank. Ask students to think of all the words they know that will fit in the blank.

4. Record all their words on a chart paper or board. When they have exhausted all words that make sense in the sentence, present the second clue.

5. Ask students which words from the list do not make sense in light of the second clue, and strike through those words.

6. Present the additional clues, and use the process of elimination to identify the Mystery Word of the Day. Allow students to decide what the final word is, based on which is the best fit for the clues.

7. Ask students to create their own definition of the word based on the clues and discussion.

Sample Mystery Word of the Day

(Bridges, 2006d)

Mystery Word Clue #1: Having a strong _____, he had no trouble climbing the mountain.

Mystery Word Clue #2: The twins' genetic _____ was remarkably similar.

Mystery Word Clue #3: In Washington, D.C., _____ Avenue is a major east-west street running just north of the United States Capitol.

Mystery Word Clue #4: The U.S.S. _____ was a 44-gun frigate that was one of the first three naval ships built by the United States; it won brilliant victories over British frigates during the War of 1812 and is without a doubt the most famous ship in the history of the United States Navy.

Mystery Word Clue #5: The Bill of Rights is the first 10 amendments to the U.S. _____.

ABC Graffiti

What is ABC Graffiti?

ABC Graffiti is a strategy to stimulate creative thinking about possible vocabulary words on a topic, unit, or piece of content (Ricci & Wahlgren, 1998) by challenging students to find related vocabulary words for each letter of the alphabet.

Why use ABC Graffiti?

It's fun! And the brain can't pay attention to anything that is boring. ABC Graffiti stimulates student thinking and helps them to make connections between prior knowledge and new information.

How do I use ABC Graffiti?

There are unlimited uses of this strategy to get students to use words. It can be used at the end of each lesson on a topic as closure, or in small groups at the beginning of a unit to assess prior knowledge. Individual students can keep lists during the unit; as they hear, read, or learn about the topic, they add new words that they think are essential. At the end of the unit, students share their individual lists and use them to write summaries. What follows is a short overview of the process for a single lesson.

1. Pass out a sheet with the alphabet listed on it from A to Z. Students can work independently for about 3 minutes to list all the words they know about a topic that go with each letter of the alphabet.

2. Organize students in groups, and ask them to create a group list. Next, students look through their material to see if they can find additional words to add to their chart.

Sample ABC Graffiti:
Space Exploration

A Astronauts	M Moon
B	N NASA
C Challenger	O Orbit
D Discovery	P Politics
E Exploration	Q Quest
F Flag Waving	R Sally Ride
G John Glenn	S Shuttle
H Hubble Telescope	T Tourist Tito
I ISS	U USSR
J January 28, 1986	V Voyager
K Kennedy Space Center	W
L Lift offs & landings	X, Y, Z

Vocabulary Rubric

What is the Vocabulary Rubric?

The Vocabulary Rubric directs students to reflect on vocabulary words and analyze how much they know about them.

Why use the Vocabulary Rubric?

Students have so many words to learn that it is impossible to spend the same amount of time on each word. It is also not necessary, so this rubric gives students and teachers an opportunity to see which words need the most instruction.

How do I use the Vocabulary Rubric?

1. Explain the rubric to the students, then give the list of vocabulary words. Use the reproducible form on page 135, or have students draw their own rubric.

2. Ask students to independently place each word in the column that best represents their knowledge of the word.

3. Collect, analyze, and use the results to prioritize your instruction to focus on the words that need the most instruction.

Vocabulary Rubric: How Well Do I Know These Terms?

(Adapted from Words, Words, Words *by Janet Allen [Stenhouse, 1999].)*

First, write down the words for this activity under "Word List." Then read the words silently. Afterwards, write each word under the heading that best describes what you know about it.

Clueless	Heard of It/Don't Know It	I Think I Know	Expert!

Word List:

Vocabulary Graphic Organizer

What is a Vocabulary Graphic Organizer?

A Vocabulary Graphic Organizer is a three-column chart that helps students to develop their own definitions of new terms from subject area classes, create graphic representations of the definitions, and record new insights. The example on page 137 was designed by Robert Marzano (2004) to be included in an academic vocabulary notebook kept by students for each subject area.

Why use a Vocabulary Graphic Organizer?

This provides a structure for students to practice steps 2 and 3 of Marzano's (2004) six steps of instruction, in which students describe the meanings of new terms in their own words and create a visual that represents the term. It helps put vocabulary words and meanings into students' long-term memory.

How do I use a Vocabulary Graphic Organizer?

1. Introduce the new term. Then ask students to write the new term on their graphic organizer or in their academic notebook and rate their knowledge of the word. Provide students with descriptions, explanations, or an example of new terms essential to developing a conceptual understanding. Tell a story, read an excerpt from the newspaper or other source, or use pictures to explain the meaning. Use simple, concrete language students understand rather than reading a dictionary definition, and try to connect their prior knowledge to the new word.

2. Ask students to think of how they can take the information and define each vocabulary word with their own descriptions. Students describe the term in their own words and write their description on the graphic organizer or in their academic notebook.

3. In the next step, students look at their descriptions and create visuals that represent their definitions. Drawing a symbol or graphic has a powerful impact on long-term memory.

4. As you go through the process with the class, using games and providing time for students to write and talk about the word meanings, students add any new insights about the words to the organizer.

Vocabulary Graphic Organizer

(Adapted from Building Background Knowledge *by Robert Marzano [Association for Supervision and Curriculum Development, 2004].)*

Term	In My Own Words Description	What I Picture	AH HA!

Semantic Feature Analysis

What is Semantic Feature Analysis?

Semantic Feature Analysis is a graphic organizer used to identify the similarities and differences of a group of items or terms.

Why use Semantic Feature Analysis?

This strategy helps students to comprehend word meanings and concepts by comparing and contrasting the word's features to those of other words with similar or opposite meanings (Johnson & Pearson, 1984).

How do I use Semantic Feature Analysis?

1. Select a general category of study, such as sports or animals. Create a matrix for key vocabulary terms or concepts; write those terms down the left side of the matrix. Direct students to copy the matrix in their notebooks as you create it.

2. List several words that fit the category in the first column, and elicit other words from students.

3. List features that the words might share across the top of the matrix, and invite students to add to this list.

4. Instruct students to mark a plus sign (+) or a minus sign (-) in each column to indicate whether or not the words listed down the left column match that feature. (A simple rating system [1, 2, 3] may also be used.) Students use a question mark if they don't know if a word has a feature or not.

5. Students explain the reasoning of their marks to other students.

Science Example of Semantic Feature Analysis

Science Terms	Plant Cell?	Animal Cell?	Plant and Animal Cell?
Cell wall	+	-	+
Cell membrane	+	+	+
Nucleus	+	+	+
Vacuole	+	+	-
Chloroplast	+	-	-
Cytoplasm	+	+	+
Golgi complex	+	+	+
Ribosome	+	+	+
Mitochondria	+	+	-
Lysosome	+	+	+

Teacher's Vocabulary Checklist

This checklist (summarized from Blachowicz & Fisher, 2002) is a way to reflect on and assess your vocabulary lesson plans and instruction. It can serve as a guide to designing lessons that increase vocabulary development.

Read the elements of effective vocabulary instruction, and check off those elements that you will try. Identify specific vocabulary for the following strategies.

1. I show enthusiasm for words and word learning.

_____ I use daily Read-Alouds.

_____ I include a Mystery Word of the Day or Word Activity of the Day.

2. I provide a word-rich environment.

_____ I use word charts and posters that exhibit student input.

_____ I use books on words and word play.

_____ I use word games.

_____ I provide time for independent reading of self-selected books.

3. I model, support, and develop good strategies for learning vocabulary.

_____ I provide rich, varied, and engaging instruction on content-area vocabulary.

_____ I use mapping, webbing, and other graphics to show word relationships.

_____ I offer multiple exposures and chances to see, hear, write, and use new words.

_____ I provide time for student practice and use of strategies.

4. I use varied assessments.

_____ My assessments differ depending on the learning goal.

_____ My assessments differ depending on the entry knowledge of the learner, and I provide specific feedback to individual students.

Reflection and Application

Review the strategies in this chapter for teaching and learning vocabulary, and select three to five strategies that you plan to try. Begin by thinking about your existing lessons. Which strategy can you add to an existing lesson plan? You may also want to think about identifying specific standards or objectives with which you will use the strategies. Alternatively, what tool can you change or modify for your classroom?

Teacher Tools	What do I NOT want to try?	How can I add this to an existing lesson?	What different standards can I use it with?	What tool can I change or use another way?
Direct Vocabulary Instruction				
Read-Alouds				
Sustained Silent Reading				
Anticipating Words				
Teaching Word Parts				
The Frayer Model				
Concept Maps				
Concept Sorts				
List, Group, Label				
Linear Array				
Mystery Word of the Day				
ABC Graffiti				

Teacher Tools	What do I NOT want to try?	How can I add this to an existing lesson?	What different standards can I use it with?	What tool can I change or use another way?
Vocabulary Rubric				
Vocabulary Graphic Organizer				
Semantic Feature Analysis				
Teacher's Vocabulary Checklist				

Notes for lesson planning:

Chapter 5

Writing to Learn

> *Learn as much by writing as by reading.*
>
> *—Lord Acton*
>
> *Meaning making is not a spectator sport. Knowledge is a constructive process; to really understand something each learner has to create a model or metaphor derived from that learner's personal world. Humans don't get ideas, they make ideas.*
>
> *—Art Costa*

Several years ago, we received a call for help from a small school in a large suburban district. The school had been tagged "underperforming"; only 40% of the students passed the state achievement tests. The school received a grant for professional development, and the principal wanted us to help her close the gap between current instructional practices and research-based practices. Our data-digging classroom observations found that teachers relied on whole-class instruction, worksheets, minimal reading, and little or no reflective talk or writing about what students had read. After sharing our data with the faculty, we facilitated a goal-setting session and helped the staff identify the focus for their school-based professional development. The teachers decided they needed to learn more about how to increase time spent reading and writing, and how to connect the two in ways that would increase comprehension of all content areas.

We started with workshop sessions where we modeled comprehension and writing to learn strategies, charging teachers with intersession assignments.

Department teams targeted writing and reflection strategies to try in their classrooms and collaboratively designed lessons. For example, in teaching science, teachers asked students to write content summaries, questions about their reading, and responses to various prompts to increase student ability to explain information and deepen their comprehension.

The principal supported the teachers' implementation of writing and reflection strategies by scheduling periodic meetings during the school day. Teachers came to the work sessions with samples of student work that represented below average, average, and above average performance. The principal duplicated one teacher's samples for each session, enabling the group to analyze the student writing to determine what the student had learned, what the student needed, and what instruction the teacher needed to provide next.

Student writing and comprehension improved over the yearlong project. Teachers learned and applied writing and comprehension strategies, and they also learned to use data to improve learning. By analyzing what students had written, they articulated their expectations for writing across grades. They were able to draft rubrics for each grade and subject and so created shared expectations and guidelines for assessing student performance.

Writing-to-learn activities can increase learning and comprehension when content teachers take a writing break from instruction to ask students to write about what they are thinking—to write their questions, connections, big ideas, and predictions. In order for students to transfer learning into long-term memory, they must do something with what they are reading, hearing, or viewing—and students must put the ideas they are learning into their own words.

The strategies in this chapter are not formal writing activities such as research papers, for which students take a topic through the formal writing process. Rather, these writing-to-learn strategies are intended to be used during instruction, in short writing breaks that allow students to spontaneously explore their thinking and quickly write an unedited draft of what they are learning.

Suggested Resources

Daniels, H., Zemelman, S., & Steineke, N. (2007). *Content area writing: Every teacher's guide.* Portsmouth, NH: Heinemann.

Flynn, R. M. (2007). Collaborating with students on an original script. In *Dramatizing the content with curriculum-based readers theatre, grades 6–12.* Newark, DE: International Reading Association.

Fulwiler, B. (2007). *Writing in science: How to scaffold instruction to support learning.* Portsmouth, NH: Heinemann.

Gallagher, K. (2006). *Teaching adolescent writers.* Portland, ME: Stenhouse.

Indrisano, R., & Paratore, J. (2005). *Learning to write, writing to learn.* Newark, DE: International Reading Association.

Ogle, D., Klemp, R., & McBride, B. (2007). *Building literacy in social studies: Strategies for improving comprehension and critical thinking.* Alexandria, VA: Association for Supervision and Curriculum Development.

Ray, K. W. (1999). *Wondrous words.* Urbana, IL: National Council of Teachers of English.

Did You Know?

- ♦ When students use writing to learn, they clarify their thinking, learn deeper content knowledge, improve thinking skills, and commit content to short- and long-term memory.

- ♦ Teaching students how to summarize text increases their comprehension and retention of content material.

- ♦ Interactive note-taking activates the learner's curiosity and anticipation, and increases the likelihood that content will be stored in short- and long-term memory.

- ♦ Inquiry activities that integrate writing engage students in analyzing immediate concrete data, and developing ideas.

- ♦ Using models of writing provides students with opportunities to read, analyze, and emulate models of good writing.

Writing High Five

What is a Writing High Five?

Writing High Five is a selected list of quick-write strategies to incorporate writing across all content areas. English and language arts teachers possess a large arsenal of writing strategies; other content teachers should have at least "a high five" of strategies that are easy to use and promote student learning!

Why use Writing High Five?

Writing activities will increase student engagement and comprehension of content material by having students put what they are learning into their own words. The real-world techniques used in these activities stimulate motivation to write and learn content.

How do I use Writing High Five?

1. Identify your topic of study.

2. Scan the following list to see what writing-to-learn activity would be most relevant for the content.

> ## Mathematics Writing Activities That Interpret Data
>
> Describe procedures by writing in the margin (Marginalia).
>
> Create diagrams and timelines: Explain in writing.
>
> Keep a journal for vocabulary and notes.
>
> Explain formulas.
>
> Make comparisons: Write how terms are alike and different.

Science Writing Activities That Create Data

Conduct experiments and keep a written log.

Take notes and write key science vocabulary in a journal.

Record observations.

Summarize theories.

Hypothesize.

Social Sciences Writing Activities for Gathering Data

Conduct interviews: Write questions and responses in a journal.

Create timelines.

Keep diaries.

Write poems.

Create ads.

Response Cards

What are Response Cards?

Response Cards collect student responses to teacher prompts. Students reflect on what they learned and give feedback to the teacher on what they need.

Why use Response Cards?

Response Cards are very easy to use. They provide manageable amounts of timely and useful feedback for a minimal investment of time. For students, they can spark reflection, application, and discussion of content learned; for the teacher, the feedback informs future instruction.

How do I use Response Cards?

You can use index cards or sticky notes for these writing prompts. Completed cards are best for class discussion, since they can be collected, shuffled, and redistributed to participants without disclosing the identity of the writer. Seven variations on Response Cards follow.

Response Card Strategy #1: The RSVP Card

Give students small, blank index cards. Assign or let students choose one of the following prompts:

- **A connection** between the day's content and what students learned the previous week

- **A question** about the content of the day's class

- **A definition** for a key concept

- **An advertising slogan or song title** that the student really likes

- **An opinion** about something the student feels strongly about

- **A solution** to a classroom or school problem

- **A fact** that really struck the student

- **A hypothesis** about an experiment or research project

- **A preference** for learning in your class

- **An answer** to a test question you've provided

Response Card Strategy #2: Entry Slip

Select one of the Response Card suggestions listed earlier. Give students an index card with the prompt written on it (or ask students to write in the prompt). Instruct students to bring the completed card to class on a specific date—it will be their "Entry Slip."

Response Card Strategy #3: The 1-Minute Paper

Stop the class 2 or 3 minutes early, and ask students to respond briefly in writing to the following two questions:

1. *What was the most useful or meaningful thing you learned during this class?*

2. *What question(s) remain uppermost in your mind as we end this session?*

Collect their responses and spend 5 minutes of the next class discussing them.

Response Card Strategy #4: The Muddiest Point

Determine what you want the students to reflect on. Reserve a few minutes at the end of class and ask students to reflect on a specific piece of content. Ask:

What was the "muddiest point" of this topic today? This week?

Collect their written replies, determine what you need to reteach or review in the next class, and respond to the students' feedback at the beginning of the next class.

Response Card Strategy #5: Reaction Sheet

This is a fun writing prompt that will engage every student because not many teachers give students an opportunity to respond in such a way to content. First, identify a segment of the lesson to which students will react. Then ask students to fold a sheet of paper into four sections and to label them as shown. Students write answers in each box to the following prompts, then they tear their responses and share them on the Data Wall. Students compare responses for similarities and differences.

What put you to sleep? Why?	What is still confusing?
An "ah ha!"	How will you use this information?

Response Card Strategy #6: The 3-2-1 Response Card

Select a content segment, then design the activity around a skill or concept you want students to learn. Ask them to identify:

♦ Three key things they have to know to understand the topic

♦ Two questions they still have about the topic

♦ One thing they'd tell someone about the topic

Response Card Strategy #7: The Writing Reflection

The Writing Reflection encourages thinking about thinking. Assign a daily reflective question around the content during the last week of the grading period, and use the responses in student conferences.

Sample Math Writing Reflection

Think about yourself as a mathematician!

Monday	Write two things you would want someone to notice about you as a math student.
Tuesday	Describe the strategies that you have learned these 9 weeks in math.
Wednesday	Describe how you can use what you have learned in math in the real world.
Thursday	Write about what you find most difficult in math. What can I do to help you?
Friday	Write a letter home that describes you as a math student this marking period.

Strategy 5.3

_____

Interactive Note-Taking

What is Interactive Note-Taking?

Interactive Note-Taking minimizes the note-taking to essential information, thus scaffolding students' note-taking skills (Burke, 2001).

Why use Interactive Note-Taking?

The adolescent learner needs a lot of support in order to learn how to organize. It is very hard for adolescents to listen to new material, decide what is key information, and write it on a piece of paper. Interactive Note-Taking helps the student focus on what is important; the student fills in blanks while at the same time listening to the majority of the lecture in order to make sense of the new material.

How do I use Interactive Note-Taking?

1. Select the essential content you want students to learn.

2. Create a handout with all the key ideas in sentence format, leaving one or two of the key words in each sentence blank.

3. Make a color-coded answer key as an overhead or PowerPoint slide. Use two different colors to help students see the visual clues and to discriminate one answer from another. For example, if you have a lecture with 15 blanks for answers, then alternate the color of each answer: Odd answers will be black, and even answers will be green.

4. Distribute the handout, and tell the students that it contains key information and that as you lecture, the key words will be on the overhead as you embellish the key points. The written answers provide support for students as they listen to the lecture and see the answers projected.

5. Cover all the answers except the ones you are discussing so the students do not go ahead or get confused.

6. When the lecture is completed, have the students review their answers and do a Cooperative Learning or Partnered Learning activity from pages 32–34.

Three-Column Journal

What is a Three-Column Journal?

The Three-Column Journal is a structure for taking notes that emphasizes rewriting information gleaned from listening to the teacher's lecture or from reading a text into the student's own words.

Why use a Three-Column Journal?

The three-column system helps students organize and retain important information. The Three-Column Journal emphasizes application of information or content learned into a personal context and increases comprehension.

How do I use a Three-Column Journal?

1. Tell students to divide their journal pages into three columns labeled as followed:

    ♦ *Notes, Facts, & Quotes*

    ♦ *Reflections, Reactions, & Observations*

    ♦ *Graphic Representation*

2. Ask students to use the *Notes, Facts, & Quotes* column for taking notes and writing your instructions, ideas from the textbook, quotes, vocabulary, and so on.

3. Ask students to use the *Reflections, Reactions, & Observations* column to record their personal reactions to lecture notes and their observations of what they learned. Specify that students are to do the following:

    ♦ Use language specific to the content area.

    ♦ Underline key concepts or vocabulary words.

    ♦ Write a minimum of three to five lines for each reflection or reaction.

4. Ask students to draw a graphic representation of the information in the final column such as a drawing, diagram, or web.

Strategy 5.5
_____

Quickwrites in Journals

What are Quickwrites in Journals?

Quickwrites are short pieces of writing in response to reading; they vary from a sentence or phrase to several paragraphs in which students make their thinking visible. Students respond in writing to a selected topic of study or more specifically to a line or segment of text that they have read (Rief, 2003). Quickwrite prompts can range from "Write what you know about the topic" to "What are the most important ideas?" to "Write a summary of what you learned today."

During this assignment, the students may make personal connections to the material they are studying; think about, learn, and begin to understand course material; collect observations, responses, and data; or practice their writing— before turning in work or being graded.

Why use Quickwrites in Journals?

Many students struggle to get their thinking on paper because they believe they can't write. Giving students an effective prompt and a short period of time to write will help students to break through the writing barriers. Student quickwrites give teachers insight into what the students are learning or not learning and also provide more information on students' thinking. Writing the connections made between new knowledge and what is already known helps learners to better comprehend new information.

How do I use Quickwrites in Journals?

Ask students to use loose-leaf notebooks for this work. Suggest that students divide their journals in several sections: one for your course, one for another course, and another for private entries.

1. Ask students to select a line or two from the text, and have them write the lines in their journals. (Alternatively, assign a line.) Tell students they have about 3 or 4 minutes to write what comes to mind.

2. Ask students to do short journal writes in class; write with them and share your writing with the class. Since you don't grade journals, the fact that you write, too, gives the assignment more value.

3. Provide time for students to share what they have written. If a student does not like what they have written, he or she may pass. Sharing the

writing gives credibility to a nongraded assignment and can include volunteers reading only, all students reading one sentence to the whole class, or each student sharing with a partner.

4. Count, but do not grade, student journals. Students must be allowed to take risks, and good journals should count in some quantitative way, such as:

   ♦ Earning a certain number of points

   ♦ Earning a "plus" added to a grade

   ♦ Serving as an in-class resource for taking tests

5. Do not write a response to every entry; it will burn you out. Instead:

   ♦ Skim-read.

   ♦ Collect journals once a week, and ask students to "star" the entry to which they would like you to respond.

6. At the end of the term, ask students to put in page numbers, a title for each entry, a table of contents, and an evaluative conclusion. This synthesizing activity asks journal writers to treat these documents seriously and to review what they have written over a whole term of study.

Strategy 5.6

Cognitive Journal Writing

What is Cognitive Journal Writing?

Journals serve as tools for capturing learners' thinking related to concepts they are studying in the content area. They help students make personal connections to the material and practice writing before engaging in formal writing such as reports. Cognitive Journal Writing engages students in six levels of thinking, comprehending, and metacognition: 1) observing important ideas and summarizing; 2) asking questions; 3) speculating, predicting, or hypothesizing; 4) reflecting on self-awareness; 5) digressing or inventing; and 6) synthesizing (Macomb Regional Literacy Training Center, 2003).

Six Cognitive Levels to Engage in Journal Writing

1. **Observation:** Describing facts and important ideas, summarizing, and interpreting details and ideas

2. **Questioning:** Writing questions about points of confusion or interest to try to make sense of the text; "how" and "why" questions

3. **Speculation:** Predicting the meaning of events, issues, facts, readings, and patterns; making interpretations; identifying problems and solutions; taking risks without fear of penalty

4. **Self-Awareness:** Thinking about one's thinking during reading in relation to the content, including writing about personal perspectives, stands on issues, differences in opinions, and reflections on personal identity

5. **Digression:** Connecting seemingly unrelated pieces of thoughts to the key idea; making inventive personal connections and explaining thinking and the divergent connections to the key topic

6. **Synthesis:** Pulling ideas together, finding relationships, or connecting one topic with one another; making connections across multiple texts

---

Why use Cognitive Journal Writing?

Teaching adolescents to be thinkers requires that they engage in metacognition, or thinking about their thinking. Cognitive Journal Writing prompts, aligned with comprehension strategies or cognitive levels, can increase comprehension of course content. Reaching the six cognitive levels provides a predictable structure that promotes student confidence and competence while providing choices of one of six levels to focus a journal entry.

How do I use Cognitive Journal Writing?

1. Teach each cognitive level, one at a time, by reading a page of text and providing an example of a journal entry on a transparency.

2. Then ask students to read a textbook passage or other text and practice the identified cognitive level in their journal.

3. Have students choose a level after a reading assignment or independent reading and create a journal entry.

For small collaborative group work, organize groups of six students, and have them number off 1 through 6. Assign the corresponding cognitive level to students; for example, have all the 1's write an observation entry.

Alternatively, ask students to select one of the levels and write on a sticky note about the content learned in class. All the students who selected the same level get together and summarize their responses. Students may report out to the whole class or post their summary journal entries on the Community Learning Wall.

RAFT

What is RAFT?

RAFT stands for Role, Audience, Format, and Topic (Buehl, 2001). RAFT is a writing technique that considers all the important elements of writing and allows students choices in their responses to learning. RAFT encourages creative thinking and motivates students to demonstrate understanding in a nontraditional, yet informative, written format. RAFT activities encourage students to think about what they are learning from another angle and to apply new knowledge in a meaningful context.

R Role of the writer: Who or what are you? How will I react to the topic from my perspective?

A Audience for the writer: To whom or what are you writing and trying to persuade?

F Format of the writing: What form will your writing assume—for example, text message, letter, song?

T Topic of the writing: What are you writing about, and what information must be shared?

A student defines each aspect of the RAFT, as in the following example.

Role:	Student	Audience:	2099 citizens
Format:	Letter in time capsule	Topic:	Most important event

I am a middle school student, and I am enclosing a letter in a time capsule for citizens in 2099 about the most important events going on in our world today.

Why use RAFT?

Although the writing that students create in RAFT is not a traditional essay, it still requires students to process information and ideas that the teacher wants them to learn—while allowing students to add personal touches and creativity to their learning.

How do I use RAFT?

1. Tell students that all writers must consider various aspects before every writing assignment, including role, audience, format, and topic. Tell them that they are going to structure their writing around these elements. Display the elements on chart paper or a bulletin board for their reference, or use the handout on page 159.

2. Display a completed RAFT example, and discuss the key elements.

3. Demonstrate and "think aloud" another sample RAFT exercise. Involve the class in brainstorming additional topic ideas. List student suggestions for roles, audiences, formats, and strong verbs associated with each topic.

4. Determine the structure or form of the writing by adding a strong verb to the topic (such as *persuade, explain, sequence, compare and contrast,* or *describe*).

5. Assign students to pairs or small groups of four to five students, and have them work together to collaborate on a RAFT organizer. Specify the topic that is related to the unit of study.

6. Circulate among the groups to provide assistance as needed. Make sure that student writing is grounded in the content being studied while allowing students to exercise creativity. Then have the groups share their completed assignments with the class.

7. After students become more proficient in developing this style of writing, have them generate RAFT assignments of their own based on current topics studied in class.

RAFT Graphic Organizer

Role

You may take on the role of yourself or another person, or you may take on the role of something inanimate—something that doesn't have life-like qualities.

Format

Experiment with a variety of formats such as telegrams, wanted posters, letters, diary entries, obituaries, epitaphs, and brochures. Explore the possibilities. Don't restrict yourself to one format!

Audience

The audience you are writing for can vary tremendously. Variation in audience requires a variation in the format and level of language you use!

Topic

Topics need to relate to the role and audience selected. Make sure your topic fits who you are trying to be as well as your audience.

The Writing Task

Social Science RAFT Example

(Bridges, 2006g)

Role	Audience	Format	Topic
writer	publisher	book jacket	subject of your novel
artist	museum curator	CD cover	topic studied
adventurer	general public	travel brochure	area explored
scientist	U.S. president	informative pamphlet	West Nile virus
reporter	environmental activists	editorial	stop complaining
lawyer	jury	closing statement	*Miranda v. Arizona*
gavel	judge	poem	don't be so hard on me
animal	self	diary entry	deforestation

Math RAFT Example

(Bridges, 2006b)

Role	Audience	Format	Topic
square root	whole number	love letter	explain relationship
fraction	baker	directions	to double the recipe
estimated sum	fractions/ mixed numbers	advice column	to become well-rounded
greatest common factor	common factor	nursery rhyme	I'm the greatest!
equivalent fractions	nonequivalent	personal ad	how to find your soul mate
fraction	whole number	petition	to be considered part of the family
improper fraction	mixed numbers	reconciliation letter	how we're more alike than different
a word problem	middle school students	song or poem	how to get to know me
equation	another equation	poem	the beauty of a balanced life
prime number	rational numbers	instructions	rules for divisibility
parts of a graph	TV audience	script	how to read a graph
exponent	jury	instructions to the jury	laws of exponents
zero	whole numbers	campaign speech	importance of the number zero
repeating decimal	set of rational numbers	petition	proving you belong to a set

Science RAFT Example

(Bridges, 2006e)

Role	Audience	Format	Topic
doctor	F.D.A.	letter	approval of a new vaccine
butterfly	bug collector	news column	reproduction
scientist	Charles Darwin	letter	Refute evolution theory.
raindrop	ocean	poem	Explain water cycle.
salmon	commercial fisherman	song	life cycle blues
nerve cell	the brain	rap	Demand that the brain listen to your pain.
zygote	friends	travelogue	Describe your journey from one cell to a multicellular organism.
DNA molecule	mRNA	commercial	Entice messenger RNA to help you transcribe and translate.
water drop	other water drops	travel guide	journey through the water cycle
bean	self	diary	process of germination
limestone rock	cave visitors	postcard	chemical weathering process
Statue of Liberty	Dear Abby readers	advice column	effect of acid rain
trout	farmers	letter	effect of fertilizer runoff
red blood cell	lungs	thank-you note	journey through the circulatory system

Strategy 5.8
_____

Cubing

What is Cubing?

In Cubing, students answer questions that are sorted into six areas (representing the six sides of a cube) to collect their thoughts and ideas before beginning to write (Cowan & Cowan, 1980). It promotes higher level thinking and increases comprehension of content. The six sides of the cube correlate to six levels of thinking and comprehension, structuring student writing on a topic from six points of view.

Six Sides of the Cube

1. **Remembering:** Tell or draw what you recall about this topic.

2. **Understanding:** Summarize the key ideas of the topic.

3. **Applying:** Demonstrate how you could use this in a new situation.

4. **Analyzing:** Sort the parts and determine how all fit together.

5. **Evaluating:** Take a stand. Argue for or against it and justify.

6. **Creating:** Produce a story, song, or poem about the topic. (National Research Center on the Gifted and Talented, 2007)

Why use Cubing?

Many students experience trouble throughout the writing process but especially in starting to write. Cubing simplifies writing for students by providing a structure that includes questions that students use to focus their thinking and writing. Cubing helps students in sustained writing for reviewing material and in essay writing. Cubing can be used for any topic in any content area and promotes comprehension and critical thinking.

How do I use Cubing?

1. When introducing Cubing, identify a simple but engaging topic, and model the strategy for the whole class using a small cube or box with the six levels written on the sides. If students need additional support, include a sample question or clue for each level on each side, or create a poster for the Community Learning Wall to which students can refer.

2. After modeling, select another topic. Toss or pass the box to a student, and ask the student to give a response for one of the sides. Continue passing the box, encouraging students to respond to different levels.

3. Next, give each student a pattern for making a three-dimensional cube (see below).

4. Assign a topic, and ask students to write a short answer to each question on the six sides of the cube. You may also provide a handout with directions for the student to use to write out some ideas for each of the six sides.

5. Finally, tell students to use their answers to write a paragraph for each of the six perspectives.

	Remember It How big is it? What color is it? What shape is it? Where can you find it?	
Understand It What does it make you think of? What do you hear? Taste? Smell?	**Apply It** What does it look like? What can it do? How could you use it?	**Analyze It** How is it made? What is it made of? Where does it come from?
	Evaluate It What is good about it? What is bad about it? Why do you like it? Why don't you like it?	
	Create It Create a slogan about it. Write a poem about it. Plan a PowerPoint show on it.	

Strategy 5.9

Give One, Get One

What is Give One, Get One?

Give One, Get One is a writing activity to use before starting a new unit of study. A brainstorming activity, it asks students to write all that they know about the topic being studied, then to talk with a partner to add to their lists of written information.

Why use Give One, Get One?

This prewriting activity helps students reflect on what they already know about a topic and gives the teacher an assessment of prior knowledge before introducing a topic. It engages students in writing and talking about a topic with partners, and is a fast-paced activity.

How do I use Give One, Get One?

1. Have students fold a piece of paper lengthwise to form two columns and write *Give One* at the top of the left-hand column and *Get One* at the top of the right-hand column.

2. Have students brainstorm a list of all the things they already know about the topic they will be studying, writing the items down in the *Give One* column.

3. After they make the list, have the students talk to other students about what is on their list in the *Give One* column.

4. Ask students to write any new information they get from these discussions in the *Get One* column of their lists, along with the name of the person who gave them the information.

5. Once everyone has given and gotten information, engage the whole class in discussion about the information students have listed.

6. Again, have students write any new information they get from this discussion in the *Get One* column.

Exit Tickets

What are Exit Tickets?

Exit Tickets are tools that encourage students to reflect and write about content they have learned.

Why use Exit Tickets?

Exit Ticket responses provide teachers with a quick and easy assessment of student learning and interest at the closure of a lesson. The information is useful in planning the next lesson.

How do I use Exit Tickets?

1. Create one or more questions or prompts for your Exit Ticket. You may write these to address comprehension strategies such as making connections, identifying the important ideas, and asking questions.

2. Ask students to respond on 3 x 5 cards, sticky notes, or printed cards. If sticky notes are used, ask students to post them on chart paper on the classroom door as they leave.

3. Read the responses, and note common patterns as well as individual needs to be addressed in the next lesson.

4. Be sure to open the next lesson with a summary or response to data gleaned from the Exit Tickets.

Exit Ticket

I thought about how the different ideas about _____ connect. We should remember that . . .

It relates to real life in that . . .

Exit Ticket

The most important ideas in today's lesson are . . .

One question I have is . . .

Strategy 5.11

Think, Write, Tear, Share

What is Think, Write, Tear, Share?

Think, Write, Tear, Share is a comprehension assessment that engages students in identifying key ideas, writing a summary, and making an oral presentation using a cooperative group structure (Clingman, 2001).

Why use Think, Write, Tear, Share?

Think, Write, Tear, Share helps students practice using several comprehension strategies. It improves comprehension and retention of ideas and concepts, and integrates reading, writing, speaking, and listening.

How do I use Think, Write, Tear, Share?

1. Select a piece of relevant text; use easy, short text when you use this for the first time with students.

2. Create a graphic organizer or four-squared worksheet with predetermined numbered questions, such as illustrated below.

3. Tell students they will be responsible for finding the most important ideas in the text. Students read the text independently, noting key ideas by highlighting, underlining, using sticky notes, or another method of your choice.

4. Give students the handout, and ask them to independently **write** brief phrases to answer the question in each square.

5. Organize students in groups of four, and ask them to number off 1, 2, 3, 4 and remember their number. Ask students to fold the paper into four squares, then open and tear along the creases to obtain four separate squares. Students redistribute the squares so that group member #1 has all of the #1 squares, the #2 student has all #2 squares, and so on.

6. Students scan the content of the squares and then think about a short synthesis that summarizes all of the ideas.

7. Students **recite** the summary statements within the group of four.

8. Representatives from each group may share summary statements with the whole group. Any student may add to or challenge a summary, citing evidence from text.

Question #1	Question #2
What is the most important idea in this chapter?	How does what you learned in this chapter connect to everyday life?
Question #3	Question #4
What are two key vocabulary words, and what do they mean?	What is one question you think will be on the quiz?

Strategy 5.12

Found Poems

What are Found Poems?

Found Poems (Worthy, Broaddus, & Ivey, 2001) is a technique for writing poems using an excerpt from a selected text such as a textbook, article, or trade book. The process requires that students identify strong words in a passage and use those words to create a poem. Poems created by students are "found" inside text written by other authors and usually emphasize the most important ideas and words in the selected text.

Why use Found Poems?

Many students struggle to create an original piece of writing. They need models and scaffolds for writing. Found Poems help students appreciate beautiful language and powerful words and provide a structure for writing.

How do I use Found Poems?

1. Select one or two paragraphs from a story or trade book that describe a character or setting. Explain that students will write a "Found Poem" using key words and phrases they find in the selected text. You may read the Found Poem at the end of this section as an example to help students understand.

2. Model the process with an excerpt from the textbook, newspaper, trade book, or magazine. Enlarge and project the text, highlight or circle key words, and delete unnecessary words. Then write your Found Poem, demonstrating how to create a line break for poetry.

3. Ask students to create Found Poems by looking for about 50 or more strong, interesting, elegant, "power" words—including verbs and nouns. Direct students to circle the strongest words and to cross out unnecessary or repetitive words. Tell students:

   Keep the words in the author's order, and write a poem using the strongest words.

   Think about the meaning of the poem.

   Consider how many words to chunk together, where to make line breaks, and which words can be emphasized through repetition.

4.   Ask students to edit and check their poems for verb tense and meaning, and to give their poems titles.

5.   Finally, students write the final draft and cite the original source (author, title, publication information, page numbers).

Example of a Found Poem: Excerpt from *I Will Fight No More Forever* by Chief Joseph

Tired of fighting,

Chiefs killed, old men all dead

Children freezing,

No food.

Hear me, I am tired

I will fight no more forever.

Reflection and Application

Review the strategies in this chapter for writing to learn, and select three to five strategies that you plan to try. Begin by thinking about your existing lessons. Which strategy can you add to an existing lesson plan? You may also want to think about identifying specific standards or objectives with which you will use the strategies. Alternatively, what tool can you change or modify for your classroom?

Teacher Tools	What do I NOT want to try?	How can I add this to an existing lesson?	What different standards can I use it with?	What tool can I change or use another way?
Writing High Five				
Response Cards				
Interactive Note-Taking				
Three-Column Journal				
Quickwrites in Journals				
Cognitive Journal Writing				
RAFT				
Cubing				
Give One, Get One				
Exit Tickets				
Think, Write, Tear, Share				
Found Poems				

Notes for lesson planning:

Appendix

Stacking the Deck for Literacy Learning

Louanne Clayton Jacobs

When teachers know how to model and support literacy in their subject areas, they create an environment conducive to helping students achieve fluency.

I've spent the past decade as a reading specialist in a middle school; a regional reading specialist serving 37 elementary, middle, and high schools; and finally as a staff development coordinator serving 11 school districts and a college professor preparing undergraduate education majors. In the capacity of reading specialist, I have conducted countless workshops and seminars for grade levels, departments, and entire faculties on the topic of literacy. As a staff development coordinator, I continue to conduct workshops but also coordinate professional development for a region with 11 school districts. As a college professor, I teach reading methods courses to undergraduate students.

I began to notice that no matter how many workshops I conducted on the topic of literacy, there was always another request. Although my staff development office provides more professional development in the area of literacy than in any other area, literacy remains at the top of each school and school system's yearly professional development request lists. Although preservice teachers take a number of reading and literacy-related classes, they continue to indicate that they feel inadequately prepared to meet the literacy needs of their students during their first year of teaching. I wondered why. Why the constant demand for literacy-related professional development? Why the feelings of inadequacy? What needs exist that are not being met?

I believe that I have discovered the answers to these questions by listening to others' questions. When I conduct workshops, a portion of each session is devoted to questions and answers. Often, participants ask about situations unique to their school or district; equally as often, their questions are universal for all schools and districts. I began to keep a list of commonly asked literacy questions. I added the questions I fielded from school and district staff development specialists and those of undergraduate students during their intern experiences. I noticed that the commonly asked questions developed into a pattern—in essence a larger question: How can teachers take all of the individual pieces of the literacy instruction puzzle they receive in their training and put those pieces together into a cohesive instructional framework, particularly a framework for content-driven middle level and high schools?

Literacy instruction, especially at the middle and high school levels, often seems overwhelming, particularly to content-area teachers who may have taken one reading course as part of their preservice preparation. Secondary teachers and administrators are under ever-increasing pressure not only to prepare students for high-stakes content assessments but also to teach literacy skills. For most, teaching the seemingly discrete components of literacy instruction (e.g., fluency, decoding, comprehension, and vocabulary development) appears not only daunting but also of less significance than content. Is there a critical mass of literacy instruction that must be reached in order to be successful at the middle and high school level? As one principal so aptly asked after a recent seminar, "What do we need to include in our instructional plan in order to stack the deck in favor of literacy for our students?" My answer is that teachers must:

- Know the learner.

- Match instruction to students.

- Understand the unique literacy demands of content areas.

- Understand the essential nature of literacy.

- Make the invisible visible.

- Create an environment that nurtures literacy.

Know the Learner

A coach would never plan a game strategy without analyzing the strengths and weaknesses of his own team and the opposing team. An actor would never take to the stage and expect to be successful without some knowledge of the audience to whom he was playing. Neither should a school develop a literacy plan without understanding the unique nature of the students for whom the plan is developed.

I recently conducted a districtwide seminar for teachers of grades 6–9. The first activity was to write statements describing a typical student on strips of overhead transparency. Some of the descriptors included, "social butterflies," "confused," "self-conscious," "unorganized," "need movement," and "outside doesn't match inside." Such statements raised gales of laughter, cries of agreement, and were often shouted aloud along with a student's name. While the exercise was a fun one and served as a nice icebreaker, it also illustrated a point: We are teaching individuals with unique personalities and traits. It's simple to look at state and national assessments and notice, for example, that students seem to be weak in identifying main idea and detail. It's more difficult to look at our students and ask, "So how do we plan to teach main idea and detail to these social, confused, self-conscious, disorganized students who look like adults on the outside and react like children on the inside?"

Match Instruction to Students

Certain instructional tools are better matched to the unique developmental needs of middle level and high school students. If we know, for example, that our students require social interaction yet are terribly self-conscious, an instructional plan that relies solely on whole-class instruction and requires students to "perform" in front of the class would not be appropriate. A better instructional approach would be to structure classes so essential literacy skills are taught in small groups where social interaction is fostered in a more emotionally secure atmosphere. Secondary schools offer the perfect opportunity to incorporate guided reading groups, for example, into an instructional plan.

If assessments reveal that our students lack depth in their vocabulary development, a number of instructional strategies can meet the academic need and build on developmental demands. Word sorts, concept maps, and other graphic organizers encourage students to develop connections among words and concepts while building upon the kinesthetic nature of adolescent learners (Blachowicz and Ogle, 2001). These tools can also be used as the basis for developing organizational strategies for these most disorganized learners, thus getting both academic and developmental bang for a single buck.

Understand the Unique Literacy Demands of Content Areas

Middle level and high school content-area teachers often ask questions that reveal their feelings of frustration when it comes to teaching literacy. They say that they feel perfectly confident teaching their subject but unprepared to teach reading or other literacy skills. And their feelings are perfectly justifiable. Content-area teachers should not teach literacy—they should support literacy within their content areas. This is not only what they should do, but what our students need them to do.

A biology teacher knows, for example, that the way a science textbook should be read is unlike the way a novel should be read. There are illustrations, headings, bold words, and other text features that should be attended to prior to reading the body of the text itself. Many teachers know this, but do not articulate it to their students. To develop a plan for literacy instruction, content-area teachers should be given time to recognize the unique literacy demands within their own subject area and develop instructional strategies to meet those demands. A simple instructional strategy that can aid content-area teachers (especially science and social studies) is Read Around the Text (Jacobs and Jones, 1999), which encourages attention to text features.

Understand the Essential Nature of Literacy

Literacy, in its essence, is nothing more than making connections. It is the ability not only to acquire new knowledge but also to access previous knowledge and make cognitive connections, thus building new knowledge. Further, it is the awareness that such processes and connections even exist.

A few years ago I was working with a group of struggling eighth-grade readers and modeled my own questioning process aloud as I read a social studies passage to them. Each time I asked myself a question, I placed a red Post-it flag on the specific passage that prompted the question. When I found the answer to my question, I placed a green flag on the text that supplied the answer. When I finished, the class practiced using the strategy in small groups or with partners, and then practiced independently.

After a few days, students not only began to feel comfortable using the strategy but also began to enjoy it as if it were a game. I was working with a small group of students who were still having trouble holding a question in their minds while reading for the answer when the near-silence of the room was punctuated by a shout from one of my favorite students: "Damn! I get it!" This young man had numerous challenges in addition to his reading difficulties, so the fact that he had just used language inappropriate to the classroom was something I was willing to overlook. Moreover, since he had gained the complete attention of the entire class, I asked just what it was that he had gotten. He replied, "I just got this whole reading thing! I just figured out that you wanted me to be thinking while I was reading. I thought I was just supposed to be reading. This is a whole new thing, isn't it?"

This student had managed to complete almost 10 years of education (he had been retained in kindergarten and fifth grade) without understanding the essential nature of literacy. He could sound out the words but did not recognize that he was supposed to be engaging in a dialogue with the words that connected them to his own thinking to create new knowledge. I am convinced that he did not know that he was supposed to be "thinking while he was reading" because he had never seen that thinking modeled for him.

Make the Invisible Visible

If we want students to become strong, flexible, independent readers, we must learn to model our own reading processes. Since reading and other literacy processes are cognitive in nature, the processing occurs in our heads. We must learn to make that invisible processing visible for students. This is the very definition of explicit teaching. Further, explicit teaching demands that we teach students not how the text is being processed, but how we, as expert readers of our subject matter, do it. This is the essence of true modeling.

Create an Environment That Nurtures Literacy

Brian Cambourne (1995) has defined seven environmental conditions that must exist for literacy learning—or any learning—to occur: immersion, demonstration, expectation, responsibility, use, approximation, and response. If we want students to exhibit a particular type of literacy, then their environment must be rich with that literacy. If we want them to be readers, for example, they must have many rich opportunities for reading. Demonstrations must be authentic; they must lay bare not how the "thing" is done, but how the teacher does it. Expectations of literacy achievement should be implicit and explicit—teachers and administrators must really believe that all students can achieve and must transmit that belief to students. Responsibility for literacy tasks should shift gradually from teacher modeling to student-guided practice to independent practice. Practice should focus on authentic uses for the literacy skills that are relevant to the lives of young adult students. Student approximations toward a literacy goal should not only be accepted but applauded and responded to with honest feedback and continued modeling.

If we want our students to become literate, we must analyze our own literacy. We must be aware of our own processing, make that processing explicit, recognize the unique developmental needs of our students, use learning activities that meet those needs, and create an environment that nurtures learning. In this way, we stack the deck in favor of literacy learning for secondary students.

References

Blachowicz, C. ,& Ogle, D. (2001). *Reading comprehension: Strategies for independent learners*. New York: Guilford.

Cambourne, B. (1995). Toward an educationally relevant theory of literacy learning. *The Reading Teacher, 49,* 182–190.

Jacobs, L. C., & Jones, D. (1999). *Read around the text.* Unpublished. www.principals.org/ schoolimprove/read_ around.cfm

Louanne Clayton Jacobs (ljacobs@aamu.edu) is director of the Regional Inservice Center of Alabama A&M and the University of Alabama and is an assistant professor of education at Alabama A&M University, Normal, Alabama.

Self-Evaluation Checklist for Literacy Lessons

Teaching is a constant stream of professional decisions made before, during and after interaction with the students: decisions which, when implemented, increase the probability of learning.

—Madeline Hunter

Strategies	Yes	Not Yet
Before Reading: Preparing Students to Read		
Did I identify objectives—what I want students to know and be able to do?		
Did I articulate objectives to students in class in an engaging way?		
Have I previewed the text and identified key concepts and vocabulary students need to know?		
Have I selected an appropriate activity to help students connect new information to what they know?		
Have I reviewed the text's features and organizational patterns to identify supports and pitfalls for comprehension?		
Have I previewed the text and identified key comprehension strategies to teach/model in a mini-lesson or remind students to use?		
Have I selected a Power Tool to teach student comprehension?		
Would a picture book be appropriate to introduce the key concept or model a critical thinking/comprehension strategy? If so, which book?		
Have I considered the six steps to Direct Vocabulary Instruction?		
Have I decided on the appropriate grouping format for each activity: whole class, pairs, small group, and independent work?		
During Reading: Assisting Student Comprehension		
If appropriate, have I selected a graphic organizer that will help students to organize key concepts?		
Did I set a purpose for reading to guide students' comprehension?		
Have I included literacy strategies that will help my students develop a clear understanding of the key concepts?		
After Reading: Reflecting		
Have I selected post-reading activities that will require students to reflect, make meaningful connections, and apply the new information?		
Have I selected an assessment that provides feedback on learning?		
Do I provide time for students to discuss what they read?		

Guidelines for the Literacy Lesson Template

Standard Addressed	Objectives
Identify the state education standard that this lesson satisfies.	Use Anderson and Krathwohl's (2001) Bloom verbs to specify skills and information that will be learned.

Resources and Materials Needed
Include the text citation, and specify the source and page numbers of selected text, essential supplies, and other materials required.

Before the Literacy Lesson: Preparing for Understanding
Preparing students for reading and learning is the most important phase and should include: ♦ Presenting the objectives in a way that results in student understanding ♦ Connecting new information to background knowledge ♦ Creating in the learner a state of curiosity or anticipation ♦ Asking a provocative question to stimulate interest in the topic

During the Literacy Lesson: Engaging Students in the Content
Actively engage the student in the content. The teacher may do some direct teaching, *but* after the direct teaching, the students must *use* the content in a hands-on way. At any given time during the lesson, at least 25–50% of the students must be simultaneously involved in an active mode.

After the Literacy Lesson: Reflecting on Content and Process
Engage the students in reflecting on what they have read and the content and/or process of the lesson. This reflection should apply comprehension strategies and the tools for learning.

Writing Task in Response to Reading Text
Describe how you will engage students in writing about what they read.

Assessment
Plan the assessment, formal and/or informal, before the lesson to show evidence of learning. Use a number of informal assessments delivered at different stages during the lesson. Some informal assessment may occur along the way to check for understanding before continuing. Consider checklists, rubrics, logs or journals, interactive notebooks, observations, and so on.

Differentiation
Describe how you will make accommodations for diverse student needs and interests.

Literacy Lesson Template

Standard Addressed	Objectives

Resources and Materials Needed

Before the Literacy Lesson: Preparing for Understanding

During the Literacy Lesson: Engaging Students in the Content

After the Literacy Lesson: Reflecting on Content and Process

Writing Task in Response to Reading Text

Assessment

Differentiation

Examples Of Bloom Verbs
(Anderson & Krathwohl, 2001)

Remembering
Define
Memorize
Recall
List
Draw
Label
Match
Duplicate

Understanding
Describe
Compare
Demonstrate
Infer
Predict
Explain
Classify
Identify
Summarize

Applying
Calculate
Convert
Experiment
Dramatize
Illustrate
Produce
Dramatize
Solve

Analyzing
Differentiate
Question
Order
Rank
Generalize
Attribute
Survey
Form
Discriminate

Evaluating
Critique
Argue
Defend
Rank
Assess
Conclude
Select
Value

Creating
Assemble
Design
Formulate
Plan
Compose
Produce
Generate
Write

Sample Literacy Lesson
Introduction to Unit on Civil Rights Movement

State Standards Addressed	Objectives
SOL USII.8a The student will demonstrate knowledge of key domestic issues during the second half of the twentieth century by examining the Civil Rights Movement.	The student will define segregation, describe examples of segregation, and apply elements of segregation in *Teammates* to current events.

Resources and Materials Needed

- Frayer Model on a piece of chart paper
- Colored markers
- Copy of *Teammates*
- Comprehension strategy graphic organizer
- SWBS on board or transparency

Before the Literacy Lesson: Preparing for Understanding

WHAT: To introduce the Civil Rights Movement

Simulation/skit on segregation: Tell the students that everyone who is wearing any red needs to move to one corner of the classroom. Check students and pretend to write names/grades on a sticky note or in the grade book—record extra points for the day's assignment. Modify to fit students' interests (bathroom break, etc). Then, ask students how they felt. Finally, explain that the objective for the day's lesson is to describe the effects of segregation.

WHAT I will teach: A short summary of the content

Essential Knowledge—effects of segregation:

- Separate public facilities (e.g., restrooms, drinking fountains, restaurants)
- Social isolation of races
- Also SOL USII.7d: African Americans' aspirations for equal opportunities

HOW I will teach: Procedures and Strategies

Use the Frayer Model to tap prior knowledge.

Develop background on concept of segregation: What is segregation? What is it not? What are examples? Non-examples?

Introduce the picture book *Teammates,* and ask students to listen for vocabulary that describes segregation.

During the Literacy Lesson: Engaging Students in the Content

Conduct a guided Read-Aloud using the CLASS comprehension strategy graphic organizer and ask students to apply Magnificent Seven at preselected passages; vary student responses with TTYN, whole-class questions, writing, and table talk.

After the Literacy Lesson: Reflecting on Content and Process

Pair students to reflect on the story and summarize the effects of segregation on one of the characters.

Provide an example using the Somebody Wanted But So template.

Return to the chart of student responses on the Frayer and take out incorrect words or information.

Add new information from the book.

Discuss with the team, then create a definition and description of segregation (individually).

Assessment

Each student uses the information on the Frayer Model chart to write a description of segregation. Also, check the summary sentences.

Differentiation

Scan a newspaper to find a present-day example of segregation. Write a paragraph that connects today's lesson and the newspaper example.

Strategy: Make Connections

What is Making Connections?

♦ Noting what the text reminds you of while reading

♦ Making connections to personal experiences

♦ Connecting one text to another text

♦ Making connections between what you read and world events, people, or issues

Thinking During Reading

♦ *This reminds me of . . .*

♦ *This is different from . . .*

♦ *This made me remember when . . .*

Teaching Tools

♦ Use two-column note-taking to identify *What This Is About/ What This Reminds Me Of.*

♦ Read aloud a short article or poem, and ask students to write a personal response.

♦ Think Aloud while reading text to model making connections.

♦ Code the Text: text-to-self, text-to-text, text-to-world connections.

♦ Model Marginalia on enlarged text on transparency. Show connections to self, texts, world.

♦ Use the Golden Lines graphic organizer.

Make Your Own Connections!

To you: _____

_____

_____

_____

_____

_____

To another text: _____

_____

_____

_____

_____

To the world: _____

_____

_____

_____

_____

_____

What is Inferring?

♦ Reading between the lines to find answers to questions

♦ Drawing conclusions based on background knowledge

♦ Using clues in the text to make sense of what the author is saying

♦ Interpreting while reading

♦ Generating hypotheses

Tips for Students

♦ Think about what you already know about the content.

♦ Ask questions: *I wonder why, how, if . . .*

♦ Think about how background knowledge helps to answer questions.

Teaching Tools

♦ Ask students to discuss and write inferences about photographs.

♦ Use two-column note-taking to list *Text Quote/Inference*.

♦ Read aloud picture books (such as *Teammates*), and discuss themes.

♦ Read aloud from textbooks, and stop at selected points to ask students to write what they visualize and infer.

♦ Use two-column note-taking from textbook passages to list *Facts/ Inferences*.

♦ Read text using a two-column graphic organizer to show *Questions/Inferences*.

Inferring is using information in your head along with evidence in the text to predict, conclude, or generalize.

How to Infer

You need to combine background knowledge with the text to:

♦ Predict what will happen or what information you will learn.

♦ Read between the lines to find answers to questions.

♦ Use the clues to make sense of what the author says.

♦ Know what the characters mean when they speak or act.

Strategy: Infer

Power Tools for Adolescent Literacy ♦ Copyright © 2009 Solution Tree Press
www.solution-tree.com ♦ Visit **go.solution-tree.com/literacy** to download this page.

Strategy: Ask Questions

What is Asking Questions?

- Interacting with the text
- Thinking while reading
- Asking questions before, during, and after reading
- Asking questions of the author, yourself, and the text
- Monitoring comprehension and clarifying confusion

Thinking During Reading

- *What is the author trying to say?*
- *What is the most important message here?*
- *What is this part really saying?*
- *What is the big idea?*
- *Does this make sense?*

Teaching Tools

- Use sticky notes to write *Huh?* on confusing parts.
- Read aloud a newspaper passage, and think aloud questions.
- Use "question webs": Write an essential question in the center and add lines with information that helps answer the question.
- Use photographs and ask students to write questions.
- Use two-column note-taking to record *Text/Questions*.
- Read aloud picture books, and model how to ask questions while reading.
- Model Marginalia using a poem or difficult excerpt from textbook to note questions.

New Bloom's Taxonomy: Key Words for Questions

1. **Remembering**
   Define
   Identify
   Locate
   List
   Draw
   Label
   Match
2. **Understanding**
   Describe
   Compare
   Demonstrate
   Infer
   Predict
   Explain
   Classify
   Summarize
3. **Applying**
   Calculate
   Convert
   Experiment
   Dramatize
   Illustrate
   Solve
4. **Analyzing**
   Differentiate
   Question
   Order
   Rank
   Generalize
   Attribute
   Survey
5. **Evaluating**
   Critique
   Argue
   Defend
   Assess
   Conclude
   Select
6. **Creating**
   Assemble
   Design
   Formulate
   Plan
   Compose
   Write

Strategy: Determine Importance

What is Determining Importance?

♦ Identifying the big idea

♦ Extracting essential information from less important ideas

Thinking During Reading

♦ *The big idea is . . .*

♦ *The big ideas so far are . . .*

♦ *This is important because . . .*

♦ *So what?*

♦ *I can use this information to . . .*

Teaching Tools

♦ Preview the text using the THIEVES technique to scan text features.

♦ Code text on sticky notes:

√ = important information

+ = new information

s = surprising information

♦ Set purpose for reading.

♦ Use sticky notes to record three important ideas from text, then write a synthesis statement.

♦ Use graphic organizers.

♦ Use Anticipation Guides.

♦ Use Mind Maps and webs.

♦ Write gist statements.

♦ Use picture books as models for writing a summary of what is important about a concept (try *The Important Book* by Margaret Wise Brown).

Summarizing is the ability to read or listen to a text and condense it by retelling or writing only the main parts with supporting details and important facts.

How to Model Summarizing

♦ Survey the text passage, and identify three to five major topics to focus on while reading. These subheadings will become the key ideas in the summaries.

♦ Divide chart paper into three to five parts, and label the sections with subheadings. These sections provide a purpose for reading.

♦ Read the text to find information for each of the categories on the chart. Record the information in sentence form.

♦ Discuss information to identify which concepts are most important to include in the summary and to decide how to write the summary in a clear and concise manner.

♦ Write a summary from the recorded information on each part of the chart for students to read.

Solid	Liquid	Gas

Example: States of Matter

Strategy: Visualize

What is Visualizing?

♦ Creating pictures in your mind

♦ Using your senses: taste, hear, feel, touch, and smell

♦ Inferring with visual images

Teaching Tools

♦ Draw a picture.

♦ Generate mental images.

♦ Construct a graph.

♦ Create a Mind Map.

♦ Act it out.

♦ Create a physical model.

♦ Produce a graphic organizer.

♦ Engage in kinesthetic activity.

♦ Use wordless picture books to write a story.

♦ Illustrate new concepts or vocabulary.

Mind Mapping

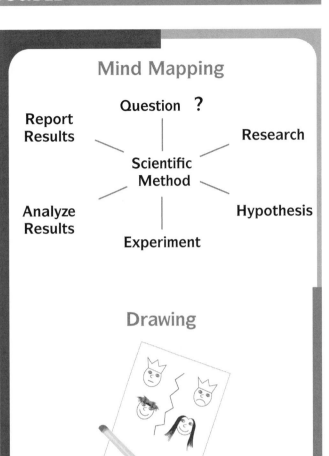

Report Results

Question ?

Research

Scientific Method

Analyze Results

Hypothesis

Experiment

Drawing

Constructing

Strategy: Synthesize

What is Synthesizing?

♦ Experiencing an Aha! or "light bulb" moment

♦ Combining information from different sources to produce a new idea

♦ Making sense of ideas during reading to create a new perspective after reading

♦ Getting the gist of the story or text

♦ Summarizing information

♦ Applying ideas and information to yourself

Thinking During Reading

♦ *I can picture . . .*

♦ *I can visualize . . .*

♦ *I can see the . . .*

♦ *I can taste the . . .*

♦ *I can hear the . . .*

♦ *I can feel the . . .*

♦ *I can smell the . . .*

Tips for Students

♦ Read multiple sources on the same topic.

♦ Find elements in common.

♦ Include your prior knowledge.

♦ Use graphics to organize.

♦ Seek additional sources.

Teaching Tools

♦ Use journal writing to note text information AND model thinking while reading.

♦ Use three-column compare and contrast: Write two concepts in the first and third column headings and "Alike" in the middle.

♦ Use two-column note-taking to show *Text Facts/My Thinking*: Write text facts in the left column and questions, connections, rewording in the right column.

Text Facts	My Thinking

♦ Model Marginalia (note-taking in margins).

♦ Use sticky notes: Write questions and then a synthesis statement at the end of a page, section, or chapter.

♦ Read aloud picture books and model thinking.

What is Monitoring & Clarifying Understanding?

♦ Thinking about your thinking while reading

♦ Realizing when meaning breaks down

♦ Using strategies to solve comprehension problems

Tips for Students

♦ Make notes of your thinking.

♦ Set purposes for reading.

♦ Make connections to yourself, texts, and the world.

♦ Make predictions.

♦ Stop and reread to clarify.

♦ Retell.

♦ Skip and read ahead to clarify.

♦ Mark confusing parts.

♦ Ask questions.

♦ Change your reading rate—slow down or speed up.

Teaching Tools

♦ Ask students to use Coding the Text symbols.

♦ Use sticky notes to record thinking and/or problems while reading

♦ Use Marginalia: Ask students to record thinking while reading in margins.

♦ Think aloud while reading to model what strategic readers do.

"Children learn to monitor themselves to keep their correct reading on track, and when something seems to be wrong they usually search for a way to get rid of the dissonance. It is important for teachers to notice self-monitoring because the process is a general one required in all reading" (Marie Clay, *Change Over Time in Children's Literacy Development,* 2001, p. 185).

Strategy: Monitor & Clarify Understanding

Think Like a Stoplight!

1. Read the directions and notice words in bold, italics, or quotation marks.

2. Read the question and all of the answers.

3. Go back and think this way about each answer:

   ♦ *This answer has nothing to do with the question or reading selection or is ridiculous, so I will stop thinking about it and give it an "R" for red, which means* Stop.

   ♦ *The answer is a possibility. It may answer the question, and it was mentioned in the text, so I will give it a "Y" for yellow, which means,* Think carefully about this answer again.

4. Reconsider the "Y" or yellow answers by going back to the reading selection to double-check.

5. Choose the best "Y" or yellow answer as your "G" or green answer, which means *Go!*

Strategy: Stoplight

Think Like a Stoplight!

Red = Stop

Yellow = Caution

Green = Go

Never answer a multiple-choice question without Thinking Like a Stoplight!

Strategy: Partners

Why Partners?

The research says collaborative learning works because:

♦ The brain is social.

♦ Fortune 500 Companies identified teamwork as the NUMBER-ONE skill of the future.

♦ It teaches social skills—important at the middle-school level.

♦ It's part of the middle-school concept.

♦ Students who learn in a cooperative model perform better academically.

♦ Positive peer relationships and interactions develop.

♦ It teaches how to work in teams.

Grouping Strategies

Ways to Group Students

♦ Use partner sign-up sheets.

♦ Cut pictures in half, and have students find their other half.

♦ Use matching stickers.

♦ Use a deck of cards! Students find the four that are alike or of the same suit for a larger group.

♦ Use Pair/Square. Students use any of the methods above to partner, then join another pair to make a foursome.

Classroom Management Techniques

♦ Flick a light switch.

♦ Play music (always the same selection).

♦ Use a silent signal such as holding your hand in the air.

♦ Create a verbal wave. Tell the group to repeat after you whenever they hear you say, "Time is up."

♦ Use a musical instrument such as a xylophone.

Picture Book Recommendations

Picture Books for Middle School Language Arts

Amelia Bedelia (all in this series)
by Peggy Parish

Caleb and Kate
by William Steig

The Fortune Tellers
by Lloyd Alexander

The Garden of Abdul Gasazi
by Chris Van Allsburg

If You Were a Writer
by Joan Lowery Nixon

The Important Book
by Margaret Wise Brown

Joyful Noise
by Paul Fleischman

Miss Alaineus
by Debra Frasier

Oh, the Places You'll Go!
by Dr. Seuss

Punctuation Takes a Vacation
by Robin Pulver

The Seven Chinese Brothers
by Margaret Mahy

Strega Nona
by Tomie dePaola

The Tale of the Mandarin Ducks
by Katherine Paterson

Teammates
by Peter Golenbock

The True Story of the 3 Little Pigs
by Jon Scieszka

Picture Books for Middle School Math

Anno's Magic Seeds
by Mitsumasa Anno

Big Blue Whale
by Nicola Davies

A Cloak for the Dreamer
by Aileen Friedman

The Greedy Triangle
by Marilyn Burns

If You Hopped Like a Frog
by David Schwartz

Math Curse
by Jon Scieszka

One Grain of Rice
by Demi

Sir Circumference and the Dragon of Pi
by Cindy Neuschwander

Picture Books for Middle School Social Studies

America the Beautiful
by Katharine Lee Bates

The Babe and I
by David Adler

Baseball Saved Us
by Ken Mochizuki

The Bracelet
by Yoshiko Uchida

The Bus Ride That Changed History
by Pamela Duncan Edwards

Can't You Make Them Behave, King George?
by Jean Fritz

The Cats in Krasinki Square
by Karen Hesse

The Coast Mappers
by Taylor Morrison

The Drinking Gourd
by F. N. Monjo

The Dust Bowl
by David Booth

Encounter
by Jane Yolen

From Slave Ship to Freedom Road
by Julius Lester

A Good Night for Freedom
by Barbara Olenyik Morrow

Going Home
by Eve Bunting

Grandfather's Journey
by Allen Say

Henry's Freedom Box
by Ellen Levine

Hiroshima No Pika
by Toshi Maruki

House Mouse, Senate Mouse
by Peter Barnes

If You Lived With the Iroquois
by Ellen Levine

Katie's Trunk
by Ann Turner

The Keeping Quilt
by Patricia Polacco

Letting Swift River Go
by Jane Yolen

The Librarian Who Measured the Earth
by Kathryn Lasky

Marshall, the Courthouse Mouse
by Peter Barnes

Molly Bannaky
by Alice McGill

My Senator and Me: A Dog's-Eye View of Washington, D.C.
by Edward Kennedy

Pink and Say
by Patricia Polacco

The Scrambled States of America
by Laurie Keller

She's Wearing a Dead Bird on Her Head!
by Kathryn Lasky

Sleds on Boston Common
by Louise Borden

Terrible Things: An Allegory of the Holocaust
by Eve Bunting

Through Grandpa's Eyes
by Patricia MacLachlan

To Fly: The Story of the Wright Brothers
by Wendie Old

The Toothpaste Millionaire
by Jean Merrill

Vote !
by Eileen Christelow

The Wall
by Eve Bunting

We the Kids
by David Catrow

Woodrow for President
by Peter Barnes

Picture Books for Middle School Science

And Still the Turtle Watched
by Sheila MacGill-Callahan

The Armadillo From Amarillo
by Lynne Cherry

Awesome Chesapeake
by David Owen Bell

Built to Last: Building America's Amazing Bridges, Dams, Tunnels, and Skyscrapers
by George Sullivan

Cook-A-Doodle-Doo!
by Janet Stevens

The Crow and the Pitcher/Professor Aesop's The Crow and the Pitcher
by Stephanie Gwyn Brown

A Drop of Water
by Walter Wick

Hot Air: The (Mostly) True Story of the First Hot-Air Balloon Ride
by Marjorie Priceman

In the Beginning
by Virginia Hamilton

June 29, 1999
by David Wiesner

Just a Dream
by Chris Van Allsburg

Kingdom of the Sun
by Jacqueline Mitton

A Log's Life
by Wendy Pfeffer

Looking at Glass Through the Ages
by Bruce Koscielniak

Mistakes That Worked
by Charlotte Foltz Jones

Now and Ben
by Gene Barretta

Plantzilla
by Jerdine Nolen

Pop's Bridge
by Eve Bunting

Rare Treasure
by Don Brown

Science Verse
by Jon Scieszka

The Water Hole
by Graeme Base

Sector 7
by David Wiesner

Weslandia
by Paul Fleischman

The Story of Clocks and Calendars
by Betsy Maestro

What's the Matter in Mr. Whiskers' Room?
by Michael Elsohn Ross

Starry Messenger
by Peter Sis

You Can't Take a Balloon Into the Metropolitan Museum
by Jacqueline Preiss Weitzman

A Subway for New York
by David Weitzman

Suggested Books for Short Read-Aloud, Think-Aloud

Mistakes That Worked
by Charlotte Foltz Jones

The Worst-Case Scenario Survival Handbook
by Joshua Piven and David Borgenicht

The Worst-Case Scenario Book of Survival Questions
by Joshua Piven and David Borgenicht

References and Resources

Abromitis, B. S. (1994, June/July). Bringing lives to life: Biographies in reading and the content areas. *Reading Today, 11,* 26.

Ackland, R. (1991). A review of the peer coaching literature. *Journal of Staff Development, 12*(1), 22–27.

Allen, J. (1999). *Words, words, words: Teaching vocabulary in grades 4–12.* Portland, ME: Stenhouse.

Allen, J. (2002). *On the same page: Shared reading beyond the primary grades.* Portland, ME: Stenhouse.

Allen, J. (2004). *Tools for teaching content literacy.* Portland, ME: Stenhouse.

Allen, D., & LeBlanc, A. (2005). *Collaborative peer coaching that improves instruction: The 2 + 2 performance appraisal model.* Thousand Oaks, CA: Corwin.

Anderson, L. W., & Krathwohl, D. R. (Eds.). (2001). *A taxonomy of learning, teaching, and assessment: A revision of Bloom's taxonomy of educational objectives.* New York: Longman.

Beck, I. L., McKeown, M. G., & Kucan, L. (2002). *Bringing words to life: Robust vocabulary instruction.* New York: Guilford.

Beck, I. L., McKeown, M. G., & Omanson, R. C. (1987). The effects and uses of diverse vocabulary instruction techniques. In M. G. McKeown & M. E. Curtis (Eds.), *The nature of vocabulary acquisition* (pp. 147–163). Hillsdale, NJ: Erlbaum.

Beers, K. (2003). *When kids can't read: What teachers can do.* Portsmouth, NH: Heinemann.

Bellanca, J., & Fogarty, R. (2003). *Blueprints for achievement in the cooperative classroom* (3rd ed.). Glenview, IL: Pearson.

Bender, E., Dunn, M., & Kendall, B. (1994). *Quick hits: Successful strategies by award winning teachers.* Bloomington: Indiana University.

Benson, B., & Barnett, S. (1999). *Student-led conferencing using showcase portfolios.* Thousand Oaks, CA: Corwin.

Biancarosa, C., & Snow, C. E. (2006). *Reading next: A vision for action and research in middle and high school literacy—A report to Carnegie Corporation of New York* (2nd ed.). Washington, DC: Alliance for Excellent Education.

Billmeyer, R., & Barton, M. (1998). *Teaching reading in the content areas: If not me, then who?* Alexandria, VA: Association for Supervision and Curriculum Development.

Blachowicz, C., & Fisher, P. (2002). *Teaching vocabulary in all classrooms.* (2nd ed.). Upper Saddle River, NJ: Prentice Hall.

Black, A., & Stave, A. (2007). *A comprehensive guide to readers' theatre.* Newark, DE: International Reading Association.

Bransford, J. D., Brown, A. L., & Cocking, R. R. (1999). *How people learn: Brain, mind, experience, and school.* Washington, DC: National Academies Press.

Bridges, C. (2006a). *Concept definition map* [Graphic organizer]. School Leadership Institute, The College of William & Mary.

Bridges, C. (2006b). *Math RAFT examples* [Graphic organizer]. School Leadership Institute, The College of William & Mary.

Bridges, C. (2006c). *Readers' theatre presentation rubric* [Handout]. School Leadership Institute, The College of William & Mary.

Bridges, C. (2006d). *Sample mystery word of the day.* School Leadership Institute, The College of William & Mary.

Bridges, C. (2006e). *Science RAFT examples* [Graphic organizer]. School Leadership Institute, The College of William & Mary.

Bridges, C. (2006f). *Social studies closed concept sort: Movements* [Graphic organizer]. School Leadership Institute, The College of William & Mary.

Bridges, C. (2006g). *Social studies example for RAFT* [Graphic organizer]. School Leadership Institute, The College of William & Mary.

Bromley, K. (2002). *Stretching students' vocabulary, grades 3–8.* New York: Scholastic.

Bromley, K. (2007). Nine things every teacher should know about words and vocabulary instruction. *Journal of Adolescent and Adult Literacy, 50*(7), 528–537.

Buehl, D. (2001). *Classroom strategies for interactive learning.* Newark, DE: International Reading Association.

Burke, J. (2001). *Illuminating texts: How to teach students to read the world.* Portsmouth, NH: Heinemann.

Burke, K. (2006, November). *Performance tasks, checklists, and rubrics: Tools for assessing standards.* Presented at the fall seminar of the School-University Research Network, Williamsburg, VA.

Buzan, T., & Buzan, B. (2006). *The mind map book: How to use radiant thinking to maximize your brain's untapped potential.* London: BBC Active.

Clingman, C. (2001). Tear and share: A cooperative comprehension check-up based on the SQ3R reading strategy. *Michigan Reading Journal, 33,* 3.

Conzemius, A., & O'Neill, J. (2001). *Building shared responsibility for student learning.* Alexandria, VA: Association for Supervision and Curriculum Development.

Cowan, G., & Cowan, E. (1980). *Writing.* New York: Wiley.

Daniels, H., & Zemelman, S. (2004). *Subjects matter: Every teacher's guide to content-area reading.* Portsmouth, NH: Heinemann.

Daniels, H., Zemelman, S., & Steineke, N. (2007). *Content area writing: Every teacher's guide.* Portsmouth, NH: Heinemann.

Davey, B. (1983). Think aloud: Modeling the cognitive processes of reading comprehension. *Journal of Reading, 27*(1), 44–47.

Desrochers, C., & Klein, S. (1990). Teacher-directed peer coaching as a follow-up to staff development. *Journal of Staff Development, 11*(2), 6–10.

Dooling, J., & Lachman, R. (1971). Effects of comprehension on retention of prose. *Journal of Experimental Psychology, 88,* 216–222.

Duke, N., & Pearson, P. D. (2002). Effective practices for developing reading comprehension. In A. Farstrup & J. Samuels (Eds.), *What research has to say about reading instruction* (3rd ed.), (pp. 205–242). Newark, DE: International Reading Association.

Dunn, S. (2006a). *Science concept sort: Physical properties* [Graphic organizer]. School Leadership Institute, The College of William & Mary.

Dunn, S. (2006b). *Science marginalia example* [Graphic organizer]. School Leadership Institute, The College of William & Mary.

Durkin, D. (1979). What classroom observations reveal about reading instruction. *Reading Research Quarterly, 14,* 481–533.

Easton, L. (2002). How the Tuning protocol works. *Educational Leadership, 59*(6), 28–31.

Feinstein, S. (2004). *Secrets of the teenage brain.* San Diego: The Brain Store.

Flynn, R. (2007). *Dramatizing the content with curriculum-based readers theatre, grades 6–12.* Newark, DE: International Reading Association.

Frayer, D., Frederick, W., & Klausmeier, H. (1969). *A schema for testing the level of concept mastery.* Technical Report No. 16. Madison: University of Wisconsin Research and Development Center for Cognitive Learning.

Fulwiler, B. (2007). *Writing in science: How to scaffold instruction to support learning.* Portsmouth, NH: Heinemann.

Gallagher, K. (2006). *Teaching adolescent writers.* Portland, ME: Stenhouse.

Gallagher, K. (2008, March). *Deeper reading in the content areas.* Presentation at the 4th Annual Adolescent Literacy Lesson Fair of The College of William & Mary, Williamsburg, VA.

Gillett, J., & Temple, C. (1983). *Understanding reading problems: Assessment and instruction.* Boston: Little, Brown.

Golenbock, P. (1990). *Teammates.* Orlando, FL: Gulliver Books.

Grasha, A., & Richlin, L. (1996). *Teaching with style: A practical guide to enhancing learning by understanding teaching and learning styles.* Pittsburgh: Alliance.

Graves, M. (2005). *The vocabulary book: Learning and instruction.* Urbana, IL: Teachers College.

Gregory, G., & Kuzmich, L. (2005). *Differentiated literacy strategies for student growth and achievement in grades K–6.* Thousand Oaks, CA: Corwin.

Gregory, V., & Rozzelle, J. (2005). *The learning communities guide to improving reading instruction.* Thousand Oaks, CA: Corwin.

Guthrie, J. T., Schafer, W. D., & Huang, C. (2001). Benefits of opportunity to read and balanced reading instruction for reading achievement and engagement: A policy analysis of state NAEP in Maryland. *Journal of Educational Research, 94*(3), 145–162.

Guthrie, J. T., & Wigfield, A. (2000). Engagement and motivation in reading. In M. L. Kamil, P. B. Mosenthal, P. D. Pearson, & R. Barr (Eds.), *Handbook of reading research: Volume III* (pp. 403–422). New York: Erlbaum.

Harste, J., Shorte, K., & Burke, C. (1996). *Creating classrooms for authors and inquirers.* Portsmouth, NH: Heinemann.

Hart, B., & Risley, T. R. (1995). *Meaningful differences in the everyday experience of young American children.* Baltimore: Paul H. Brookes.

Harvey, S., & Goudvis, A. (2000). *Strategies that work.* Portland, ME: Stenhouse.

Hollister, I., & Stone, P. (2006). *4-3-2-1 report rubric* [Handout]. School Leadership Institute, The College of William & Mary.

Indrisano, R., & Paratore, J. (2005). *Learning to write, writing to learn.* Newark, DE: International Reading Association.

Ivey, G. (2006a). *Classroom literacy assessments* [Handout]. School Leadership Institute, The College of William & Mary.

Ivey, G. (2006b). *Reading and writing interest inventory* [Handout]. School Leadership Institute, The College of William & Mary.

Ivey, G., & Fisher, D. (2005). *Creating literacy rich schools for adolescents.* Alexandria, VA: Association for Supervision and Curriculum Development.

Jacobs, L. (2003). Stacking the deck for literacy learning. *Principal Leadership.* Accessed at http://findarticles.com/p/articles/mi_qa4002/is_200311/ai_n9336228 on May 7, 2007.

Jensen, E. (1995). *Super teaching.* San Diego: The Brain Store.

Jensen, E. (2003). *Tools for engagement.* Thousand Oaks, CA: Corwin.

Johnson, D., & Pearson, P. (1984). *Teaching reading vocabulary* (2nd ed.). New York: Holt, Rinehart & Winston.

Kagan, S. (1994). *Cooperative learning.* San Clemente, CA: Kagan Publishing.

Keene, E., & Zimmerman, S. (1997). *Mosaic of thought: Teaching comprehension in a reader's workshop.* Portsmouth, NH: Heinemann.

Lamb, A. (2006a). *Math concept sort: SOL 8.2 concept sort* [Graphic organizer]. School Leadership Institute, The College of William & Mary.

Lamb, A. (2006b). *Math marginalia example* [Graphic organizer]. School Leadership Institute, The College of William & Mary.

Macomb Regional Literacy Training Center. (2003). *Michigan content literacy assessments, standards, and strategies: Grades 6-7-8 trainer of trainers.* Clinton Township, MI: Macomb Intermediate School District. Unpublished manuscript.

Marzano, R. (2004). *Building background knowledge for academic achievement: Research on what works in schools.* Alexandria, VA: Association for Supervision and Curriculum Development.

Marzano, R., & Pickering, D. (2004). *Building academic vocabulary.* Alexandria, VA: Association for Supervision and Curriculum Development.

Marzano, R., & Pickering, D. (2005). *Building academic vocabulary: Teacher's manual.* Alexandria, VA: Association for Supervision and Curriculum Development.

Marzano, R., Pickering, D., & Pollock, J. (2001). *Classroom instruction that works: Research-based strategies for increasing student achievement.* Alexandria, VA: Association for Supervision and Curriculum Development.

Marzano, R., Pickering, D., & Pollock, J. (2004). *Classroom instruction that works: Research-based strategies for increasing student achievement.* Alexandria, VA: Association for Supervision and Curriculum Development.

Moje, E. (2003, July). *Developing literacy in the content areas.* Presented at the Center for the Improvement of Early Reading Achievement (CIERA) Summer Institute, Ann Arbor, MI.

Nagy, W. E. (1988). *Teaching vocabulary to improve reading comprehension.* Urbana, IL: National Council of Teachers of English, and Newark, DE: International Reading Association.

Nagy, W. E., Anderson, R. C., & Herman, P. A. (1987). Learning word meaning from context during normal reading. *American Educational Research Journal, 24*(2), 237–270.

National Research Center on the Gifted and Talented. (2007). *Cubing and think dots.* Accessed at http://curry.edschool.virginia.edu/files/nagc_cubing__think_dots.pdf on October 9, 2008.

Ogle, D. S. (1986). K-W-L group instructional strategy. In A. S. Palinscar, D. S. Ogle, B. F. Jones, & E. G. Carr (Eds.), *Teaching reading as thinking* (Teleconference Resource Guide, pp. 11–17). Alexandria, VA: Association for Supervision and Curriculum Development.

Ogle, D., Klemp, R., & McBride, B. (2007). *Building literacy in social studies: Strategies for improving comprehension and critical thinking.* Alexandria, VA: Association for Supervision and Curriculum Development.

Palinscar, A., & Brown, A. (1984). Reciprocal teaching of comprehension: Fostering and monitoring activities. *Cognition and Instruction, 2,* 117–175.

Pearson, P. D., Roehler, L., Dole, J., & Duffy, G. (1992). Developing expertise in reading comprehension. In S. Samuels & A. Farstrup (Eds.), *What research says to the teacher* (2nd ed., pp. 145–199). Newark, DE: International Reading Association.

Pfeffer, J., & Sutton, R. I. (2000). The knowing-doing gap: How smart companies turn knowledge into action. Boston, MA: Harvard Business School.

Philp, R. (2007). *Engaging tweens and teens.* Thousand Oaks, CA: Corwin.

Pichert, J. W., & Anderson, R. C. (1977). Taking different perspectives on story. *Journal of Educational Psychology, 69*(4), 309–315. Accessed at http://eric.ed.gov/ERICDocs/data/ericdocs2sql/content_storage_01/0000019b/80/35/72/fd.pdf on October 9, 2008.

Pilgreen, J. L. (2000). *The SSR handbook: How to organize and manage a sustained silent reading program.* Portsmouth, NH: Boynton/Cook Publishers.

Piven, J., & Borgenicht, D. (2005). *The worst-case scenario book of survival questions.* Philadelphia: Quirk Productions.

Ramaprasad, A. (1983). On the definition of feedback. *Behavioral Science, 28,* 4–13.

Rasinski, T. (2003). *The fluent teacher: Oral reading strategies for building word recognition, fluency, and comprehension.* New York: Scholastic.

Rasinski, T., et al. (2000). *Teaching word recognition, spelling, and vocabulary: Strategies.* Newark, DE: International Reading Association.

Ray, K. W. (1999). *Wondrous words.* Urbana, IL: National Council of Teachers of English.

Ricci, G., & Wahlgren, C. (1998, May). *The key to know "paine" know gain.* Paper presented at the 3rd Annual Convention of the International Reading Association, Orlando, FL.

Rief, L. (2003). *100 quickwrites.* New York: Scholastic.

Robb, L. (2000). *Teaching reading in middle school.* New York: Scholastic.

Robb, L. (2003). *Teaching reading in social studies, science, and math.* New York: Scholastic.

Robbins, P. (1991). *How to plan and implement a peer coaching program.* Alexandria, VA: Association for Supervision and Curriculum Development.

Rozzelle, J. ,& Gregory, V. (2006). *A guide to facilitating teacher reflection: Improving literacy in all content areas.* Huntington Beach, CA: Pacific Learning.

Rutherford, P. (2002). *Instruction for all students.* Alexandria, VA: Just ASK Publications.

Ryder, R., & Graves, M. (2003). *Reading and learning in content areas* (3rd ed.). New York: John Wiley and Sons.

Sadler, R. (1989). Formative assessment and the design of instructional systems. *Instructional Science, 18,* 119–144.

Santa, C. (1988). *Content reading including study systems: Reading, writing, and studying across the curriculum.* Dubuque, IA: Kendall/Hunt.

Scearce, C. (2007). *122 ways to build teams.* Thousand Oaks, CA: Corwin.

Schmoker, M. (2006). *Results now: Achieving unprecedented improvements in teaching and learning.* Alexandria, VA: Association for Supervision and Curriculum Development.

Schwartz, R. (1988). Learning to learn vocabulary in content area textbooks. *Journal of Reading, 32*(2), 108–118.

Short, K., Harste, J., & Burke, C. (1996). *Creating classrooms for authors and inquirers* (2nd ed.). Portsmouth, NH: Heinemann.

Sparks, D. (1990, Spring). Cognitive coaching: An interview with Robert Garmston. *National Staff Development Council Journal, 11*(2), 12–15.

Sylwester, R. (2007). *The adolescent brain.* Thousand Oaks, CA: Corwin.

Taba, H. (1967). *Teacher's handbook for elementary social studies: An inductive approach.* Reading, MA: Addison-Wesley.

Tierney, R., Readance, J., & Dishner, E. (1995). *Reading strategies and practices: A compendium* (4th ed.). Needham Heights, MA: Allyn & Bacon.

Tomlinson, C. (2003). *Fulfilling the promise of the differentiated classroom: Strategies and tools for responsive teaching.* Alexandria, VA: Association for Supervision and Curriculum Development.

Trelease, J. (2001). *The read-aloud handbook* (5th ed.). New York: Penguin Books.

Turner, A. (1997). *Katie's trunk.* New York.: Simon & Schuster Children's Publishing.

University of Washington. (2007, March 26). Toddlers engage in "emotional eavesdropping" to guide their behavior. *Science Daily.* Accessed at www.sciencedaily.com/releases/2007/03/070326095423.htm on May 13, 2008.

Weber, E. (2003). Instructions. In *Michigan content literacy assessments, standards, and strategies: Grades 6-7-8 trainer of trainers.* Clinton Township, MI: Macomb Intermediate School District. Unpublished manuscript.

Whimbey, A., & Whimbey, L. (1975). *Intelligence can be taught.* New York: E. P. Dutton.

Wilhelm, J. (2001). *Improving comprehension with think-aloud strategies.* New York: Scholastic.

Worthy, J., Broaddus, K., & Ivey, G. (2001). *Pathways to independence: Reading, writing, and learning in grades 3–8.* New York: Guilford.

Zeno, S. M., Ivens, S. H., Millard, R. T., & Duvvuri, R. (1995). *The educator's word frequency guide.* Brewster, NY: Touchstone Applied Science Associates.

Make the Most of Your Professional Development

Let Solution Tree schedule time for you and your staff with leading practitioners in the areas of:

- **Professional Learning Communities** with Richard DuFour, Robert Eaker, Rebecca DuFour, and associates

- **Effective Schools** with associates of Larry Lezotte

- **Assessment *for* Learning** with Rick Stiggins and associates

- **Crisis Management and Response** with Cheri Lovre

- **Classroom Management** with Lee Canter and associates

- **Discipline With Dignity** with Richard Curwin and Allen Mendler

- **PASSport to Success** (parental involvement) with Vickie Burt

- **Peacemakers** (violence prevention) with Jeremy Shapiro

Additional presentations are available in the following areas:
- Youth at Risk Issues

- Bullying Prevention/Teasing and Harassment

- Team Building and Collaborative Teams

- Data Collection and Analysis

- Embracing Diversity

- Literacy Development

- Motivating Techniques for Staff and Students

Solution Tree
555 North Morton Street
Bloomington, IN 47404

(812) 336-7700 • (800) 733-6786 (toll free) • FAX (812) 336-7790

email: info@solution-tree.com

www.solution-tree.com

Focused Instruction: An Innovative Teaching Model for All Learners
Gwen Doty
Effectively respond to diverse learning styles and achievement levels with strategies and reproducible tools that will help you customize, scaffold, and layer your instruction. Reach every student in the classroom, while still holding all students accountable for learning. **BKF249**

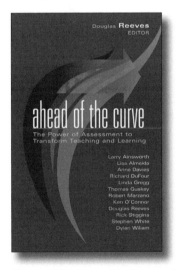

Ahead of the Curve: The Power of Assessment to Transform Teaching and Learning
Edited by Douglas Reeves
Get the anthology that offers the ideas and recommendations of many of the world's leaders in assessment. Many perspectives of effective assessment design and implementation culminate in a call for redirecting assessment to improve student achievement and inform instruction. **BKF232**

The Collaborative Teacher: Working Together as a Professional Learning Community
Cassandra Erkens, Chris Jakicic, Lillie G. Jessie, Dennis King, Sharon V. Kramer, Thomas W. Many, Mary Ann Ranells, Ainsley B. Rose, Susan K. Sparks, and Eric Twadell
Foreword by Rebecca DuFour
Introduction by Richard DuFour
Transform education from inside the classroom with this accessible anthology. Specific techniques, supporting research, and real class-room stories illustrate how to work together to create a guaranteed and viable curriculum and use data to inform instruction. **BKF257**

Pyramid Response to Intervention: RTI, Professional Learning Communities, and How to Respond When Kids Don't Learn
Austin Buffum, Mike Mattos, and Chris Weber
Foreword by Richard DuFour
Accessible language and compelling stories illustrate how RTI is most effective when built on the Professional Learning Communities at Work™ model. Written by award-winning educators, this book details three tiers of interventions—from basic to intensive—and includes implementation ideas. **BKF251**

Solution Tree Visit www.solution-tree.com or call 800.733.6786 to order.